First World War
and Army of Occupation
War Diary
France, Belgium and Germany

3 CAVALRY DIVISION
Divisional Troops
3 Field Squadron Royal Engineers
16 September 1914 - 22 May 1919

WO95/1146/3

The Naval & Military Press Ltd
www.nmarchive.com
Published in association with The National Archives

Published by

The Naval & Military Press Ltd

Unit 10 Ridgewood Industrial Park,

Uckfield, East Sussex,

TN22 5QE England

Tel: +44 (0) 1825 749494

www.naval-military-press.com

www.nmarchive.com

This diary has been reprinted in facsimile from the original. Any imperfections are inevitably reproduced and the quality may fall short of modern type and cartographic standards.

© Crown Copyright
Images reproduced by permission of The National Archives, London, England, 2015.

Contents

Document type	Place/Title	Date From	Date To
Heading	WO95/1146/3 3 Cavalry Division Divisional Troops 3 Field Squadron Royal Engineers Sept 1914-May 1919		
Heading	3rd Field Squadron R.E. Sep 1914-May 1919		
Heading	3rd Cavalry Division Sept To Dec 1914-May 1919		
Heading	Sept To Oct-1914		
War Diary	Chatham	16/09/1914	16/09/1914
War Diary	Ludgershall	17/09/1914	17/09/1914
War Diary	Aldershot	17/09/1914	17/09/1914
War Diary	Salisbury	19/09/1914	19/09/1914
War Diary	Aldershot	21/09/1914	03/10/1914
War Diary	Portsmouth	25/09/1914	25/09/1914
War Diary	Chatham	26/09/1914	28/09/1914
War Diary	Portsmouth	03/10/1914	03/10/1914
War Diary	Aldershot	03/10/1914	03/10/1914
War Diary	Ludgershall	04/10/1914	12/10/1914
War Diary	Southampton	12/10/1914	12/10/1914
War Diary	Boulogne	14/10/1914	17/10/1914
War Diary	Hazebrouck	18/10/1914	18/10/1914
War Diary	Poperinghe	19/10/1914	19/10/1914
War Diary	Passchendaele	19/10/1914	19/10/1914
War Diary	Zonnebeke	20/10/1914	20/10/1914
War Diary	St Julien	20/10/1914	20/10/1914
War Diary	Frezen Berggn	20/10/1914	20/10/1914
War Diary	Hooge	21/10/1914	21/10/1914
War Diary	Wormezeele	22/10/1914	22/10/1914
War Diary	Zillebeke	23/10/1914	24/10/1914
War Diary	Zonnebeke	20/10/1914	20/10/1914
War Diary	Ypres	21/10/1914	21/10/1914
War Diary	Zanvoorde	22/10/1914	23/10/1914
War Diary	Klein Zillebeke	23/10/1914	24/10/1914
War Diary	Zandvoorde	25/10/1914	26/10/1914
War Diary	Zonnebeke	20/10/1914	20/10/1914
War Diary	Voormezeele	21/10/1914	22/10/1914
War Diary	Klein Zillebeke	23/10/1914	26/10/1914
War Diary	1/2 Mile W of Zamvoorde	27/10/1914	27/10/1914
War Diary	Zillebeke	28/10/1914	31/10/1914
War Diary	Halte	01/11/1914	02/11/1914
Heading	3rd Field Squadron R.E. Vol III I.II-31.12.14		
War Diary	Halte M Ypres-Menin Wad	01/11/1914	04/11/1914
War Diary	1/2 Mile W of Halte	05/11/1914	06/11/1914
War Diary	Dickenbush Beck Farm	07/11/1914	22/11/1914
War Diary	Hazebrouck	23/11/1914	14/12/1914
War Diary	St Jean-Cappelle	15/12/1914	16/12/1914
War Diary	Hazebrouck	17/12/1914	31/12/1914
Heading	3rd Field Squadron RE 3rd Cavalry Division Jany-1915 To Jany 1916		
Heading	3rd Field Squadron R.E Vol IV 1-31.1.15		
War Diary	Hazebrouck	28/01/1915	30/01/1915
Heading	3rd Field Squadron RE Vol V 1-28.2.15		
War Diary	Hazebrouck	01/02/1915	02/02/1915

War Diary	Ypres	03/02/1915	13/02/1915
War Diary	Hazebrouck	13/02/1915	28/02/1915
Heading	3rd Field Squadron RE Vol VI 1-31.3.15		
War Diary	Hazebrouck	01/03/1915	20/03/1915
War Diary		18/03/1915	25/03/1915
War Diary		20/03/1915	30/03/1915
War Diary		29/03/1915	06/04/1915
War Diary		22/03/1915	31/03/1915
Heading	3rd Field Squadron R.E Vol VII 2.3.4-15.6.15		
War Diary		23/04/1915	16/06/1915
Map	Reference Zillebeke Sheet 1/10,000		
Heading	3rd Field Squadron RE Vol VIII June To Sept 15		
War Diary		06/06/1915	05/09/1915
Heading	3rd Sqd. R.E Sept To Oct Vol 9 To 10		
Heading	3rd Fil Sqdr RE September 1915-Jan 1916 Volume		
War Diary	Vincly	06/09/1915	24/09/1915
War Diary	Philosophe	25/09/1915	25/09/1915
War Diary	Loos	26/09/1915	29/09/1915
War Diary	night	28/09/1915	18/11/1915
Heading	Nov-Dec-1915 Jan-1916		
War Diary		01/07/1917	31/07/1917
Miscellaneous	A.A. & Q.M.G. 3rd Cav Div		
War Diary		04/08/1917	31/08/1917
War Diary	Field	01/09/1917	31/12/1917
War Diary		28/11/1917	03/12/1917
War Diary		01/01/1918	31/01/1918
War Diary	Flamicourt	01/02/1918	27/03/1918
Heading	3rd Field Squadron, R.E April 1918		
War Diary		02/04/1918	30/04/1918
War Diary	Sains Les Pernes	01/05/1918	08/05/1918
Diagram etc			
War Diary		17/05/1918	31/05/1918
Miscellaneous	Statement of Work Done By, III Field Troop 150v Cam. Cav. Bde		
Miscellaneous Map	Trenches Continuous.		
War Diary		01/06/1918	30/07/1918
Map	Pickets & Wire dumped to complete firm fences Also from 23rd.3.4 to 26.6.7.8		
War Diary	Bettencourt	01/08/1918	07/08/1918
War Diary	East of Amiens	08/08/1918	16/08/1918
War Diary	Bettencourt St Oeun	16/08/1918	25/08/1918
War Diary	Caumont	25/08/1918	25/08/1918
War Diary	Galametz	26/08/1918	09/09/1918
War Diary	Caumont	10/09/1918	15/09/1918
War Diary	Anmanoeuris	16/09/1918	17/09/1918
War Diary	Haravesnes	18/09/1918	24/09/1918
War Diary	An trek	25/09/1918	29/09/1918
War Diary	Coulaincourt	00/10/1918	25/11/1918
Heading	3rd Field Squadron R.E.		
War Diary		01/12/1918	17/12/1918
War Diary	Sclessin Belgium	00/01/1919	00/01/1919
War Diary	Sclessin Belgium	01/02/1919	08/04/1919
War Diary	3rd Field Squadron R.E.	01/05/1919	22/05/1919
War Diary	Sclessin	01/05/1919	22/05/1919
Heading	Huy		

(3)

WO 95/1116

3 Cavalry Division
Divisional Troops

3 Field Squadron Royal Engineers

Sept. 1914 - May 1919

1914-1919
3RD CAVALRY DIVISION

3RD FIELD SQUADRON R.E.

SEPT 1914 - MAY 1919

WAR DIARY

OF

3RD FIELD SQUADRON RE

3RD CAVALRY DIVISION

SEPT^R TO DEC^R - 1914

May 1919

SEPT.R & OCT. 1914

Army Form C. 2118.

WAR DIARY
INTELLIGENCE SUMMARY

3rd Fd. (Erase heading not required.) Sqdn. RE

Hour, Date, Place	Summary of Events and Information	Remarks and references to Appendices
16-9-14 CHATHAM	Following officers ordered by W.O. minute N°121/128 (A97) of 15-9-14 to proceed to WINDMILL HILL CAMP, LUDGERSHALL, to form 3rd Fd Sqdn RE Capt. C.E.P. Sankey RE 2/Lt R.D. Park RE " J. Kiggell RE Following officers, posted to 2nd Fd Sqdn RE, were transferred to 3rd Fd Sqdn RE Lt. J.C. Bowles RE	
17-9-14 LUDGERSHALL ALDERSHOT	Capt Sankey arrived & put in demands for equipment and leave for new unit. Proceeded ALDERSHOT and arranged with O.C. Training Depot RE as to personnel	
19-9-14 SALISBURY	Capt Sankey reported H.Q. S.C. action taken. Officers of 3rd Fd Sqdn ordered to ALDERSHOT to assist in selection and training of personnel	Appendix 1.
21-9-14 ALDERSHOT	Officers 3rd Fd Sqdn reported C.E. A.C.	

Army Form C. 2118.

(2)

WAR DIARY
INTELLIGENCE SUMMARY
(Erase heading not required.)

3rd Fd Sqdn RE

Instructions regarding War Diaries and Intelligence Summaries are contained in F. S. Regs., Part II. and the Staff Manual respectively. Title pages will be prepared in manuscript.

Hour, Date, Place	Summary of Events and Information	Remarks and references to Appendices
21-9-14 to 3-10-14 ALDERSHOT	Officers employed in training of personnel	
25-9-14 PORTSMOUTH	O.C. 3 F.S. saw DADOS 3 Cav Div, at that time ordered to assemble equipment for unit. Establishment of unit had not been finally settled and no A.F. G 1098 had been issued.	
26-9-14 to 28-9-14 CHATHAM	O.C. 3 F.S. attended meeting of R.E. Committee to decide type of light intrg. equipment to be issued to unit. Samples of equipment in RE Workshops, Captain Sankey's design, approved and forwarded to I.R.E.S. Woolwich. O.C. 3 F.S. arranged with O/c RE Records for training of personnel from nr station to complete establishment, as provisionally arranged.	
3-10-14 PORTSMOUTH	O.C. 3 F.S. saw DADOS 3 Cav Div and was informed that equipment for unit was being sent direct from WOOLWICH to LUDGERSHALL.	

Army Form C. 2118.

WAR DIARY
INTELLIGENCE SUMMARY
(Erase heading not required.)

3rd Fd Sqdn RE

(3)

Hour, Date, Place	Summary of Events and Information	Remarks and references to Appendices
3-10-14 ALDERSHOT	Telegram 3CD 39 received in evening. At this date, practically none of the sapper personnel had been dismissed Training Depot RE and in fact about half had not even arrived from former stations for their training	Appendix 2
4-10-14 LUDGERSHALL	Officers and available personnel proceeded to WINDMILL HILL CAMP. 2 hundred G.S. arrived with a Wagons, bus 2 hundred G.S., arrived with a certain amount of miscellaneous equipment — 2 Wagon G.S. were issued in lieu of 4 Carts Tool RE. These are not suitable for the purpose required, and will diminish the mobility of the unit, particularly across country.	Appendix 3
4-10-14 & 5-10-14 LUDGERSHALL	During the night 91 horses arrived. No saddlery nor harness having been received they could only be secured by their halters	Appendix 4

1247 W 3299 200,000 (E) 8/14 J.B.C. & A. Forms/C. 2118/11.

Army Form C. 2118.

WAR DIARY
INTELLIGENCE SUMMARY
(4)

(Erase heading not required.)

3rd Fd Sqdn RE

Instructions regarding War Diaries and Intelligence Summaries are contained in F. S. Regs, Part II. and the Staff Manual respectively. Title pages will be prepared in manuscript.

Hour, Date, Place	Summary of Events and Information	Remarks and references to Appendices
5-10-14 LUDGERSHALL	Telegram from ORDNANCE, WOOLWICH, attached, was first intimation that all stores detailed on AF G 1078-41B were not coming direct from WOOLWICH. As the unit did not exist in peace, it had no peace equipment at all, and C.O.O. TIDWORTH was unable to supply more than a proper proportion.	Appendix 5
6-10-14 to 12-10-14 LUDGERSHALL	Personnel, horses and equipment arrived in instalments during this period.	
5-10-14 LUDGERSHALL	2/Lt R.C.F. Dodgson reported for duty as Interpreter. Lt R.F. Young RAMC reported for duty as Medical Officer.	
11-10-14 LUDGERSHALL	2 limbered wagons G.S. RE arrived in lieu of 2 limbered wagons G.S. These vehicles are of flimsy construction & small capacity, and probably will prove not very suitable.	

Army Form C. 2118.

WAR DIARY
INTELLIGENCE SUMMARY (5)

(Erase heading not required.)

3rd Fd Sqdn RE

Instructions regarding War Diaries and Intelligence Summaries are contained in F. S. Regs., Part II. and the Staff Manual respectively. Title pages will be prepared in manuscript.

Hour, Date, Place	Summary of Events and Information	Remarks and references to Appendices
12-10-14 LUDGERSHALL	Entrainment took place in accordance with W.O. telegram 2725 QMG2 of 12-10-14	Appendix 6
14-10-14 SOUTHAMPTON 11.30 p.m.	Unit embarked S.S. CITY OF BENARES	
15-10-14 BOULOGNE 6.30 a.m.	Unit disembarked and went into camp near BASSIN EMILE LOUBET	
17 18-10-14 BOULOGNE 4.30 p.m.	entrainment completed	
18 19-10-14 HAZEBROUCK	detrained by 11.0 a.m. Proceeded by march route, via STEEN VOORDE, to POPERINGHE. Reported to H.Q. IV Corps and billetted.	
19-10-14 POPERINGHE 7.0 a.m.	Reported H.Q. IV Corps and ordered to join 3rd Cav: Dv: at PASSCHENDAELE. Proceeded by march route via YPRES and ZONNEBEKE	
11.50 a.m.	Reported arrival to H.Q. 3rd Cav Dv	Appendix 7

Army Form C. 2118.

WAR DIARY
~~INTELLIGENCE SUMMARY~~
(Erase heading not required.)

3rd Fd Sqdn   RE

Instructions regarding War Diaries and Intelligence Summaries are contained in F. S. Regs., Part II. and the Staff Manual respectively. Title pages will be prepared in manuscript.

(6)

Hour, Date, Place	Summary of Events and Information	Remarks and references to Appendices
19-10-14 PASSCHENDAELE	Unit remained in reserve until relieved to billet at ZONNEBEKE CHATEAU	
20-10-14 ZONNEBEKE	In accordance with 3 Cav Div, operation order 15, No 1 troop despatched 4.30 a.m. to join 6th Cav Bde, and No 2 troop, 5.0 a.m. to 7th Cav Bde. H.Q. & Bridging Train remained parked at ZONNEBEKE Troops remained with Bdes all day and assisted in entrenching position. No 2 troop lost 1 man wounded. Troops went into billets with their Bdes.	Appendix 8
ST JULIEN 2.30 p.m.	Information received from H.Q. 3rd Cav Div that troops should remain permanently attached to Bdes.	
FREZENBERG CM	H.Q. & Br. Tr: bivouaced by roadside.	

Army Form C. 2118.

WAR DIARY (7)
INTELLIGENCE SUMMARY
(Erase heading not required.) H.Q. & Br: Tr:

3rd Fd Sqdn RE

Instructions regarding War Diaries and Intelligence Summaries are contained in F. S. Regs., Part II. and the Staff Manual respectively. Title pages will be prepared in manuscript.

Hour, Date, Place	Summary of Events and Information	Remarks and references to Appendices
21-10-14 HOOGE 2 p.m.	Parked by roadside proceeded via ZILLEBEKE to WORMEZEELE and billeted in school, 7.0 p.m.	
22-10-14 WORMEZEELE 5.0 p.m.	Proceeded to ZILLEBEKE and billeted in convent.	
23-10-14 ZILLEBEKE	Remained in billets. O.C. 3 F.S. visited N° 1 & 2 troops	
24-10-14 ZILLEBEKE 10 a.m.	Proceeded towards YPRES, and parked on road 1/4 m. W of ZILLEBEKE VIJVER. O.C. 3 F.S. (a) started ½ Park & smaller party at work on a maxim-gun emplacement, and the preparation for a bridge for demolition at the CHATEAU between HOLLEBEKE and ZANDVOORDE (b) entrenched a position and civil labour at ZANDVOORDE	

Army Form C. 2118.

WAR DIARY
or
INTELLIGENCE SUMMARY

1st Troop (Erase heading not required.) 3rd 7d Sqdn. RE.

Hour, Date, Place	Summary of Events and Information	Remarks and references to Appendices
ZONNEBEKE 20·10·14 4:30 a.m.	1st Troop proceeded at 4:30 a.m. to report at POELCAPELLE at 5:30 a.m. to O.C. 6th Bde 3rd Cav. Div. O.C. 6th Bde. having moved at 4:30 a.m. the O.C. 1st Troop reported to him at WEST ROOSEBEKE at 6·0 a.m. The troop entrenched a supporting line for 10th Hussars until 9·0 a.m. when it withdrew into reserve for remainder of day; following 7d Ambulance into billets at YPRES at 6·30 p.m.	
YPRES 21·10·14 6·30 a.m.	1st Troop followed 1st D.G.'s to HOOGE on MENIN road where it halted till 12·30 p.m.; moving on then to ZILLEBEKE where it remained till 6·30 p.m.	(21·10·14)
ZANVOORDE 22·10·14 12·30 a.m.	The troop reached ZANVOORDE at 10·0 p.m. and occupied trenches in firing line at 12·30 a.m. 22·10·14; horses remained in ZANVOORDE.	
ZANVOORDE 23·10·14 10·0 a.m.	1st Troop remained in trenches; being relieved at 7·30 p.m. and bivouacked with H.Q. 6th Bde at KLEIN ZILLEBEKE.	

Army Form C. 2118.

WAR DIARY
INTELLIGENCE SUMMARY
(Erase heading not required.)

1st Troop. 3rd Sqdn. RE.

Hour, Date, Place	Summary of Events and Information	Remarks and references to Appendices
KLEIN ZILLEBEKE 23.10.14 10.30 am	1st Troop remained with H.Q. 6th Bde at KLEIN ZILLEBEKE	
KLEIN ZILLEBEKE 24.10.14 10.30 am	At 4.0 p.m. O.C. 1st Troop with a men dug M.G. Emplacement and prepared Canal bridge for demolition at HOLLEBEKE CHATEAU. Captured 1 Bavarian Prisoner. Remainder of Troop assisted O.C. 3rd 7? Sqdn. with trenches at ZANDVOORDE.	
ZANDVOORDE 25.10.14 10.0 pm	Troop proceeded with H.Q. 6th Bde to farm 3/4 mile from ZANVOORDE on ZILLEBEKE road at 5.0 pm. Occupied alarm trench at 10.0 pm.	
ZANDVOORDE 26.10.14 11.0 pm	Occupied alarm trench at 5.30 am. Proceeded to HOLLEBEKE CHATEAU at 2.0 pm; and rejoined H.Q. 3rd 7? Sqdn. at KLEIN ZILLEBEKE at 3.0 pm.	

Army Form C. 2118.

WAR DIARY
or
INTELLIGENCE SUMMARY

3rd Sqdn R.E. (Erase heading not required.) 2nd Troop.

Instructions regarding War Diaries and Intelligence Summaries are contained in F. S. Regs., Part II. and the Staff Manual respectively. Title pages will be prepared in manuscript.

Hour, Date, Place	Summary of Events and Information	Remarks and references to Appendices
20.10.14. ZONNEBEKE	2nd Troop attached to 7th Cav. Bde. Reported at H.Q. 7th Bde. at 5 a.m., & went to PASSCHENDAELE where we improved trenches for the guns. Retired in evening and billeted left K Battery N.T.A. at a farm near ST. JULIEN Supper Street. Kennedy wd. in leg.	
21.10.14. VOORMEZEELE 8 p.m.	Kept with K Battery all day. Billeted in cement at VOORMEZEELE.	
22.10.14. VOORMEZEELE.	Left K Battery at 6 p.m. & dug trenches for the 2nd L.G.s. South of KLEIN ZILLEBEKE. Helped men trenches when finished.	
23.10.14. KLEIN ZILLEBEKE.	Dug trenches for the "Blues" 1/4 mile further East. Slept in led-horses.	
24.10.14. KLEIN ZILLEBEKE	Improved trenches for the BLUES - head cover & latrine cricket net. Cpl Dyas knee wounded in leg by shrapnel shell thro' bloc. slit.	
25.10.14. KLEIN ZILLEBEKE.	Improved trenches. Summerley left the 2nd Life Guards & was died of pneumonia in hospital later.	
26.10.14. KLEIN ZILLEBEKE	Rejoined Squadron at 2.45 in KLEIN ZILLEBEKE. Billeted. H. Farm at ZILLEBEKE	

Army Form C. 2118.

WAR DIARY
or
INTELLIGENCE SUMMARY
(Erase heading not required.)

3rd Field Sqdn R.E.

Instructions regarding War Diaries and Intelligence Summaries are contained in F. S. Regs, Part II. and the Staff Manual respectively. Title pages will be prepared in manuscript.

Hour, Date, Place	Summary of Events and Information	Remarks and references to Appendices
26th KLEIN ZILLEBEKE	Troops rejoined Sqdn. Sqdn dug 150x of 3'x3' trench S of KLEIN ZILLEBEKE in case of a retirement. Time of digging 3 p.m. to 8 p.m. Billeted in ZILLEBEKE	
27th 2 mile W of ZAMVOORDE	Capt Sandys out and put the Sqadron on digging a line of trenches to be occupied in case of a retirement from the ZAMVOORDE ridge. After 2 p.m. 25 civilians were put to work with sapper instructions and worked very well until 6 p.m. when the Sqdn went back to ———————— a farm near by to billet. 11 p.m. the Sqdn in 4 parties entrenched the trenches on the ZAMVOORDE ridge - chest high - about 1 had cover and in some cases two lengths.	
28th ZILLEBEKE	Provost Marshall provided 82 civil labour who were employed S+S.E. of ZILLEBEKE (entirely) the line manned on 2)th morning & join hands with 2nd Cav Bde in rear of HOLLEBEKE	

WAR DIARY or INTELLIGENCE SUMMARY

Army Form C. 2118.

(Erase heading not required.)

Hour, Date, Place	Summary of Events and Information	Remarks and references to Appendices
29th Oct ZILLEBEKE	With 40 civilians & 1st Sqdn cleared the foreground of and dug trenches in a 3rd line of defence. Work done to 5 p.m. dug trench and concealed. Gave 85 yards of breastwork cleared 20" of wire fencing prepared for exchine. 50" of very thick hedge ranged. Night. 2nd Sqdn 45 strong dug 25" of 3'6" × 2'6" trench. Bivouaced and concealed & 3 officers mens shelters in rear connected by communication trenches. Also concealed tarred with 1.65 p.m. to 5 a.m. on the ZANDVOORDE ridge in 1st French line.	
30th Oct ZILLEBEKE	C.O. reported for work to Sqn Staffs at KLEIN ZILLEBEKE. Was informed that 1st line was abandoned. 2nd line held a.m. until 3 p.m. on 3rd line. C.O. off C.E.P. Scouty wounded in leg by shrapnel bullet. 200 civilians killed in rear of ZILLEBEKE until 3 p.m. when dispersed unpaid by enemy shell fire. Billetts ZILLEBEKE.	
31st ZILLEBEKE	Gutted ZILLEBEKE 8 a.m. under shell fire. 2 Lt YOUNG RAMC wounded by high explosive shell in shoulder. moved with Amm Col & Ironmachal at HALTE on YPRES – MENIN road.	
1st November HALTE	O.C. and 2nd Troops accoured at HALTE. Billetted in barn near Bridge train sent to join train 2 miles S.W. YPRES.	
2nd November HALTE	Remaining at HALTE. 1 Cony with 450 shovels sea pickets & wiring under also O.C. 3rd R.S. Bridges train with Cavaly Train shelter all night – no casualties.	

NOV + DEC

121/4027

3rd Field Squadron R.E.

Vol III. 1.11 — 31.12.14

nil

November

Army Form C. 2118.

WAR DIARY 3rd Field Squadron R.E.
or
INTELLIGENCE SUMMARY

(Erase heading not required.)

Instructions regarding War Diaries and Intelligence Summaries are contained in F. S. Regs., Part II. and the Staff Manual respectively. Title pages will be prepared in manuscript.

Hour, Date, Place	Summary of Events and Information	Remarks and references to Appendices
Nov 1 " 2 " 3 " 4 } HALTE on YPRES-MENIN road	No work done during these days, a motor lorry full of tools received on Nov 2 and bridging train sent back to off YPRES under O.C. A.S.C. for movements. Moved billets ½ mile nearer YPRES owing to shell fire.	
Nov 5 ½ mile W of HALTE	The unit was sent to 1st Corps for work. Proceeded with 26th Coy R.E. to the trenches E of HERENTHAGE chateau and dug communication trenches and shelter pits from 11p.m. to 3·30 a.m.	
Nov 6	Improved the above and cut a line through the wood for passage of troops and stretcher bearers, bridged small stream, work completed 2·15 a.m. Moved billets E of YPRES owing to shell fire.	Jeronimos N Eng Field Sqdn RE Capt [signature]
Nov 7 DICKEBUSH BECK Farm	Repaired damaged trenches in front edge of wood at HERENTHAGE, with much interference by rifle and shell fire, completed 1·30 a.m.	
Nov 8 "	Work in and around YPRES for 1st Corps repairing and improving roads filling shell holes, removing obstructions 8·a.m — 4·30 p.m. 8 a.m — 4·30 p.m. Brought lorry up to LILLEBEKE and distributed tools to units requiring them. Lorry badly ditched twice it is a 3 ton lorry and too heavy for the work.	

November

WAR DIARY 3rd Field Squadron RE.
or
INTELLIGENCE SUMMARY

Army Form C. 2118.

(Erase heading not required.)

Hour, Date, Place	Summary of Events and Information	Remarks and references to Appendices
Nov 9 DICKEBOSH BECH FARM	Reconnoitering	
Nov 10 "	Day Building shelters for 7th Bde Bivouack - 1 troop lent to 1st Div Night 300× wiring at KLEIN ZILLEBEKE 60× of new trench dug with troopers.	
Nov 11 "	Day Building shelters Night repair of trenches KLEIN ZILLEBEKE	
Nov 13.14.15.16	Construction of roofed shrapnel proof dug outs in railway cutting, 19 dug outs capable of housing 360 men. Squared timber doors, shutters and telegraph wire was obtained in YPRES Average days work as the shelters 7½	
Nov 18	Day Dug outs completed with a troop Night one troop repairing trenches at KLEIN ZILLEBEKE.	Jackson for being Nr at last John Br (cmd)

November

WAR DIARY 3rd Field Squadron R.E.
INTELLIGENCE SUMMARY
(Erase heading not required.)

Army Form C. 2118.

Instructions regarding War Diaries and Intelligence Summaries are contained in F.S. Regs., Part II. and the Staff Manual respectively. Title pages will be prepared in manuscript.

Hour, Date, Place	Summary of Events and Information	Remarks and references to Appendices
Nov 19 DICKEBUSCHBECK Farm	night work in trenches at KLEIN ZILLEBEKE especially rebuilding traverses and making machine gun emplacement, also clearing trenches and roads. Day shown work, repair of roads after work 6 p.m. – 2 a.m.	
Nov 20 "	repair of above trenches, erection of shrapnel proof shelters in same road mending	
Nov 21 "	Recalled from track to HAZEBROUCK for repair of trenches preparation to handing over to the French at 9 p.m. Collected 20 rifles & 80 shovels on leaving	
Nov 22 "	moved billets to HAZEBROUCK	
Nov 23–30 HAZEBROUCK	unit refitting	

Jensen?
Lieut RE
Cmdg 3rd Field Squadron RE

December

WAR DIARY 3rd Field Squadron R.E.   Army Form C. 2118.
of
INTELLIGENCE SUMMARY
(Erase heading not required.)

Hour, Date, Place	Summary of Events and Information	Remarks and references to Appendices
December 1 to 13 HAZEBROUCK	Refitting – Instruction given to squadron in digging trenches with head and over head cover, making huddles and bivies. Handing water carts and W/guns /technical number	
December 14 "	Proceeded to billets at ST JEAN'S CAPPELLE (9 march route)	
December 15 ST JEAN-CAPPELLE	—	
December 16	Proceeded to billets at HAZEBROUCK (9 march route and R.H.Q)	
December 17 – 24 HAZEBROUCK	Erection of timber stables for Erren [?] horses, and repair of water carts and W/guns	
December 26 – 31 "	A factory for trench guns & grenade-making established for experimental and instructional purposes. Repairs to water carts and W/guns.	

J.C. Snowden
Lieut. R.E.
Comg. 3rd Field Squadron R.E.

WAR DIARY

OF

3RD FIELD SQUADRON R.E.

3RD CAVALRY DIVISION

JANY. 1915 TO JANY. 1916

099
0798
M.T 2

121/44447

3rd Cavalry Division

3rd Field Squadron R.E.

Vol IV. 1 — 31.1.15

January

Army Form C. 2118.

WAR DIARY
or
INTELLIGENCE SUMMARY.

3rd Field Squadron
3rd Cav Div
January 1915

(Erase heading not required.)

Instructions regarding War Diaries and Intelligence Summaries are contained in F. S. Regs., Part II. and the Staff Manual respectively. Title pages will be prepared in manuscript.

Hour, Date, Place	Summary of Events and Information	Remarks and references to Appendices
HAZEBROUCK	The Squadron did not take part in any operations during this month.	
	Repairs were carried out to the horse vehicles and water carts of all units in the division	
	One aeroplane shed was built for 2nd Wing R.F.C. near	
MORBECQUE		
	The Officers, N.C.O's and men were of 3rd Cav Div were instructed in the machinery of bombs, hand grenades and trench mortars and practised in using them.	
	The instruction took the form of 3 lectures of 2 hours each daily given to officers of the squadron 9-11 11-1 & 2 & 4	
	During the month the Squadron assisted the training of the division by day & night in lieu of digging & the erection of wire entanglements.	
	Some experiments were carried out in digging & clearing trenches	
Jan 28-29 30	Instruction in the use of hand grenades and bombs was given to officers & men of 28th Infantry Division	

J.E. Edmonds
Capt R.E.
Cmdg 3rd Field Squadron
R.E.

3rd Cavalry Division

3rd Field Squadron RE.

Vol V 1 – 28.2.15.

Army Form C. 2118.

WAR DIARY 3rd Field Squadron Royal Engineers
or
INTELLIGENCE SUMMARY.
(Erase heading not required.)

February 1915

Hour, Date, Place	Summary of Events and Information	Remarks and references to Appendices
HAZEBROUCK February 1st	Packing stores for move Capt. L.C.T. reach wounded in leg	
2	Two troops in 3 motor lorries moved to YPRES. 2 tow carts 1 water cart 3 local wagons, one motor lorry filled with tools forwarded to YPRES & billetted there	
YPRES 3	Officers of the squadron visited trenches while held by the French 7th Sqdn. manufactured hand grenades – mud screws – wire hurses. 30 x of French wire just out by 2nd Troop	
4	Sqdn proceeded to the trenches at dusk with stores. 2nd troop installed itself in the line. 1st Troop brought up & placed stores	a/Sgt Watson killed
5.6.7.8	2nd Troop wiring in the trenches – draining & paving floors – repairing banquets – putting up wire in front. 1st Troop making stores for 2nd troop – bringing stores & returning up to the trenches	
9.10.11.12.13	Similar work. 1st Troop in the trenches – 2nd troop making stores bringing up & stores & returns	
11th 9 p.m	Moved out of billets owing to shell fire – returned at 10.30 p.m.	

WAR DIARY of 3rd Field Squadron Royal Engineers

INTELLIGENCE SUMMARY

Army Form C. 2118.

(Erase heading not required.) February 1915

Hour, Date, Place	Summary of Events and Information	Remarks and references to Appendices
February 13 night HAZEBROUCK	Proceeded en bloc to billets near HAZEBROUCK	
February 14.15.16.17	Repairs to wagons and water carts of 3rd Cavalry Division. Refitting - billets in practice trenches.	
18th	The Squadron was ordered to YPRES to assist the 28th Div. in work on their trenches. Both troops without horses or wagons moved to YPRES in motor lorries and billeted here. 1st Troop put out wire along part of the line.	
19th	Officers reconnoitred trenches in the morning. Capt Bowles killed. At night 2nd Troop put up wire in front of trenches.	
20th	No work done owing to rifle attack. At night Both troops out wiring and drawing & improving trenches.	
21st, 22nd	Whole Squadron at work on shelters for 200 men. By day 1 Officer & 10 men supervised Infantry digging party; by night remainder of Squadron carried on work.	
23rd, 24th, 25th		
26th	Squadron left YPRES on motor buses at 2.0 p.m. arriving in billets at HAZEBROUCK at 4.15 p.m.	
27th, 28th	Repairs to wagons of 3rd Cav. Div. carried on; men washing and refitting.	

151/4893

3rd Cavalry Division

3rd Field Squadron R.E.

Vol VII 1 - 31. 3. 15

WAR DIARY
or
INTELLIGENCE SUMMARY
(Erase heading not required.)

Army Form C. 2118.

W.H. Sim........Captain, R.E.
O.C. 3rd Field Squadron R.E.

March 1915 (1st Sheet)

Hour, Date, Place	Summary of Events and Information	Remarks and references to Appendices
HAZEBROUCK March 1st–9th	Unit remained in billet at HAZEBROUCK. Repairs to horsed transport of 3rd Cav. Div. carried out during the month.	
March 7	Capt. V.H. Simon joined unit and took over command.	
3–9	Working parties of from 200–400 men (from 3rd Can. Div.) employed on digging a line of trenches about 2 mile long situated west of STEEN BECQUE. This formed part of a reserve line constructing by cavalry.	
	Worn in CRE Indian Corps. The Officers and NCOs & men of 3rd Fd Sqdn assisted watching hostile safeguard the cavalry.	
7–9.	No 2 troop under the 2Lt Kiggell practiced use of rafting equipment, lend rafting & spar bridge.	
10–16	In immediate readiness to move, while fighting in progress at NEUVE CHAPPELLE and ST-ELOI.	
17.	Moved to BOIS-DE-NIEPPE in readiness, returning in the evening.	
	Moved to LE SART, 1 Mile W. of MERVILLE, returning in the evening.	

Army Form C. 2118.

........[signature]........
Captain, R.E.
O.C. 3rd Field Squadron, R.E.

WAR DIARY
or
INTELLIGENCE SUMMARY.
(Erase heading not required.)

March 1915   (2nd Sheet.)

Hour, Date, Place	Summary of Events and Information	Remarks and references to Appendices
March 18–20	Work in trenches near STEEN BECQUE completed.	
18–25	Short courses of instruction carried out for both troops, including use of rafter equipment, crossing drill, knotted roping, trestle bridging, and mining. Map reading carried out from time to time during the month, and recapitulation of explosives and demolitions.	
20–30	8 men under O.C. Cavalry Corps Signals at LA MOTTE. Experiments made in listening for sounds of mining with several [spaced?] instruments.	
March 29 – April 6	3 detachments of 1 officer & 3 other ranks from 7th Cav. Bde. — 6 — — — 8 — — trained in use of trench mortars.	

WAR DIARY
or
INTELLIGENCE SUMMARY

O.C. 3rd Field Squadron R.E.
........Capitain, R.E.

Army Form C. 2118.

March 1915 (3rd Sheet)

Hour, Date, Place	Summary of Events and Information	Remarks and references to Appendices
March 22-26	1 Offr & 3 ORs each regiment of demolitions with explosives.	
27-31	1 Offr & 3 ORs from each regiment of 6" and 8" Cav. Bdes. trained in demolitions with explosives. During last week of March an increase of establishment of the unit has been authorised, Me establishment being changed from { 1 Major (a Captain) 3 Subalterns, 2 troops, with 1st line & holding tram, 1 & 8 wagons, to { 1 Major, 1 Captain, 4 Subalterns & 4 troops, with 1st line & holding tram of 6 & 6 wagons. The necessary reinforcements, wagons, horses & stores were demanded.	

3rd Cavalry Division

8rd Field Squadron. R.E.

Vol VII — 2.3.4 — 15.6.15.

W.H. Shain......Captain, R.E.
O.C. 3rd Field Squadron R.E.

Army Form C. 2118.

WAR DIARY
or
INTELLIGENCE SUMMARY. April 1915 [1st sheet]

(Erase heading not required.)

Instructions regarding War Diaries and Intelligence Summaries are contained in F.S. Regs., Part II. and the Staff Manual respectively. Title pages will be prepared in manuscript.

Hour, Date, Place	Summary of Events and Information	Remarks and references to Appendices
April 23/15 24 - 29	3rd Cav. Div. moved to near VLAMERTINGHE & 3rd Field Squadron remained with division till 29th. The division been in reserve to the area west of YPRES & moving about in varying degrees of readiness, sometimes hourly & sometimes dismounted	
29.	3rd Field Squadron placed at disposal of PLUMER'S force. In the evening moved the Squadron and tool carts to position on west end of BELLEWAARDE LAKE. No horse lines during there & sending all horses back to Camp C 1½ miles S. of VLAMERTINGHE. In evening made machine gun emplacements on 3 roads running N. and E. from WIELTJE.	
30	Continued 3 support points N and E of WIELTJE By Gen. John Vaughan selecting the sites and supplying with men from his brigade of 2nd Cav. Div.	

(73989) W4141—463. 400,000. 9/14. H.&J.Ltd. Forms/C. 2118/10.

Army Form C. 2118.

WAR DIARY
or
INTELLIGENCE SUMMARY.

(Erase heading not required.)

W.H. Ham .... Captain, R.E.
O.C. 3rd Field Squadron R.E.

May 1915 [1st Sheet]

Instructions regarding War Diaries and Intelligence Summaries are contained in F.S. Regs., Part II. and the Staff Manual respectively. Title pages will be prepared in manuscript.

Hour, Date, Place	Summary of Events and Information	Remarks and references to Appendices

May 1st

Completed the 3 above mentioned suffocating trenches to N and E of WIELTJE & constructed a fourth one. Horses in camp C shelled & moved to farm in G.24.a. N.1 OUDERDOM. – One horse killed & 1 wounded, 3 sick men in but subsequently recovered from 120 Battery R.F.A.

2 Unit Handed over to C.R.E. 28 Division. Cooperation with 1st Fd. Sqdn R.E. We wired 800x of new line of trenches running N & S through FREZENBERG. This is the line on to which one infantry retired on the 3rd.

3 Withdrew sappers, tools carts to G.24.a., farm N.1 OUDERDOM.

4 Cleaning up. Working under C.E. 5 Corps. "PLUMER'S" Force, constructing trenches from PORTE de HENIN to canal junction North of YPRES, with mixed infantry parties of about 300 every night. A 4th experiment in a hut just dealt in tallow just J. work in tattered scratchy manner.

5–7

WAR DIARY
or
INTELLIGENCE SUMMARY.
(Erase heading not required.)

O.C. ...J.H.Ewin... Captain, R.E.
3rd Field Squadron R.E.

Army Form C. 2118.

May 1915 [2nd Sheet]

Instructions regarding War Diaries and Intelligence Summaries are contained in F.S. Regs., Part II and the Staff Manual respectively. Title pages will be prepared in manuscript.

Hour, Date, Place	Summary of Events and Information	Remarks and references to Appendices
May 8.	Returned to HAZEBROUCK by march route to rest.	
9.	3rd Cav. Div. returned to position & reachan[?] west of VLAMERTINGHE by motor bus. 3rd Fd Sqdn returned to same G 24 A. No. 1 OUDER DOM by march route.	
	PM returned horses lorry wagons 14/7 ZILLEBEKE under 2 lines Traverse, & supplies per troop horses left to look after the riding horses.	
9 – 11	Thin list of about 15 Rank & file only tsop troops on 1st Fd Sqn in the trenches along Co-operation with takings over the positions from PORTE YPRES canal junction N. of YPRES once more de MENIN to position 1,600 x within the hostile infantry within position at night.	
12	3rd Cav. Div. ordered to hold trenches from HOOGE to railway by this line accommodated by daylight with myself by segments of fifteen of the division. I who intended 3rd Cav. Div. to NA the lost moment. V	

(73989) W.4141—463. 400,000. 9/14. H.&J.Ltd. Forms/C. 2118/10.

WAR DIARY or INTELLIGENCE SUMMARY

Army Form C. 2118.

O.C. 3rd Field Squadron R.E.

May 1915 [3rd sheet]

Hour, Date, Place	Summary of Events and Information	Remarks and references to Appendices
May 12	Hill from BELLEWAARDE LAKE up to YPRES - VERLOREN HOEK road, consequently the ground to North of roadway was not permitted to be developed either by RE or by regimental officers. This order was not adhered to unless absolutely necessary. In some cases men of 3rd Cav. Div. officers to have been a very grave error & his undoubtedly responsible for a portion of the very heavy casualties sustained by the division the following morning. Furthermore, the 3rd Fan Sunken has allowed to continue until then height of YPRES was kept line 1 trenches. These deficiencies the 3rd Cav. Div. of the use of these own RE at a critical juncture. On this night I without orders took two companies J and routes to construct (1) a communication trench to rear Bellewaarde of BELLEWAARDE - PAR(?) & (2) a look farm N. of a portion of their front trench. The 7th Bde who took over when Railway work to road afforded by RE on artillery attack but V Corps.	

Army Form C. 2118.

V.H.S___ Captain, R.E.
O.C. 3rd Field Squadron R.E.
May 1915   4th Sheet

WAR DIARY
or
INTELLIGENCE SUMMARY.
(Erase heading not required.)

Hour, Date, Place	Summary of Events and Information	Remarks and references to Appendices

May 13th

3rd Cav. Div. men heavily shelled shortly after dawn and troops forced to evacuate trenches between railway and YPRES-VERLOREN HOEK road., falling back to parallel track about 800x west.

Reported to POTEITJE chateau at 8 P.M. & Mj. Gen BRIGGS instructed me to co-operate with Northumberland Fus. & R.E. [Major Podmore D.S.O] enroll 800 men of D.L.I. & establish best possible line of trenches between ruins & VERLOREN HOER road. There was some delay in collecting the working parties & tools, but we succeeded in digging a rough line of trenches as required, working from about 11.30 P.M. till 2 A.M. There was no proper patrol to our front while we worked, but the German infantry showed little initiative & He went no carried out with practically no interference.

Army Form C. 2118.

WAR DIARY
or
INTELLIGENCE SUMMARY.
(Erase heading not required.)

V.H.Simon .... Captain, R.E.
O.C. 3rd Field Squadron R.E.
May 1915 [5th sheet]

Hour, Date, Place	Summary of Events and Information	Remarks and references to Appendices
May 14.	3rd Cav. Div. relieved by 2nd Cav. Div. 3rd Fd. Squadron cooperating with 2nd Fd Sqn in work 2 sections from behind line of trenches dug on 13th, and 2nd Fd Sqn consolidated the trenches dug on 13th, carrying the line further forward.	
15 – 17	Resting at OUDER DOM. Cavalry Force established under Gen. BYNG.	
18.	Drew tools from R.E. advanced park, VLAMERTINGHE. To replace those lost by the brigades, + completed the divisional reserve of tools carried in motor lorry. Instructed the minium in use of the new MILLS hand grenade. Major SANDYS DSO., actg CRE Cavalry force, having over 3rd Fd Sqn to look after trenches of 9th Cav Bde. [Bt. Gen. GREENLY] on look south of MENIN ROAD at HOOGE. 2 Lieut Ruggell + myself carefully reconnoitred the line on night 18-19 whilst 9th Cav Bde. took over from 82nd Bde. [1st A.& S. Hrs & Scots Fus.]	

Army Form C. 2118.

WAR DIARY
or
INTELLIGENCE SUMMARY.
(Erase heading not required.)

L.H. Sm........ Captain, R.E.
O.C. 3rd Field Squadron R.E.
May 1915. (6th Sheet)

Hour, Date, Place	Summary of Events and Information	Remarks and references to Appendices
May 19.	at night with return party of 150 men we consolidated the front line of trenches in J.13.C. & also wired the MENIN road east of HOOGE strongly.	
20.	As above, also improved line in front in J.13.C. and helped form at J.18.a.3-5 for occupation by 14th Q⁷ 9° Cav. Bde. Also dug a communication trench across MENIN ROAD at J.18.b.4.5	
21st–25th	Worked with 9° Cav. Bde. as above.	
22.	1st Fd Sqdn. took over trenches at HOOGE. 3° Fd Sqn. resting.	
23.	Major Sanders handed over 3° Fd Sqdn. to work with 1st Cav. Bde. [Bt. Gen. E. Makins] in trenches from J.13.C. to J.24.b. I reported to Gen. Makins at midday, leaving Maroush obtained all information & a sketch from Major FRY OC 2nd Wessex Fd. Co. RE. After dusk 2 Lieut PARK & myself reconnoitred the trenches & I made following report.	

Army Form C. 2118.

WAR DIARY
or
INTELLIGENCE SUMMARY.
(Erase heading not required.)

May 1915 (7 sheets)

O.C. 3rd Field Squadron R.E. ....Witham.... Captain, R.E.

Hour, Date, Place	Summary of Events and Information	Remarks and references to Appendices

May 23.

extract from report

to GOC 1st Cav. Bde.

--- (3) Some of the hand grenades in the trenches are damp & require re-fuzing. Please collect them all & place together at dumping place by 10 P.M. & R.E. will re-fuze them. They should then be re-distributed in empty bully-beef or ammunition boxes. 50% in firing line & 50% with supports.

(4) The Germans are sapping. I am probably wrong, in front of your trenches about 150× from your left end and about 60× to your front; O.C. 17th Hussars Gr RE is starting a counter mine, but in moving from shovel got torn next in the action addition to the hypernia, I also intend to try to delay the Germans, & also intend them to throw hand grenades into what is going on, & to the ascertain the end of Ypres salient.

10.30 PM Witham Capt RE
23/5/15.

WAR DIARY or INTELLIGENCE SUMMARY

Army Form C. 2118.

V H Sun — Captain, R.E
O.C. 3rd Field Squadron R.E. May 1915. (8° sheet)

Hour, Date, Place	Summary of Events and Information	Remarks and references to Appendices

May. 24.

Sent 2ⁿᵈ troop (2/Lt Taggett) to École de Bienfaisance, with orders to proceed up to the trenches & carry out certain work & to lay out tapes for a trench in rear of the present threatening by German operations, did carry to the German having developed a strong attack at H100 G.E. & having captured trenches between H100 G.E. and BELLE WAARDE · LAKE and in J.13.C. the Brig. Maj. 1st Cav. Bde ordered him to return to his billets as the work was not carried out.

On 2/Lt Taggett's return I proceeded myself to the École & reported to the Cav. Station at 11-30 p.m. when Major Sandys, act. CRE Cav. Corps ordered him to return to billets, having been relieved by 2ⁿᵈ Cav. Div. on 1st Cav. Div. having night 24-25 kn to be carried on RE work in the RE of V corps.

Army Form C. 2118.

WAR DIARY
or
INTELLIGENCE SUMMARY.
(Erase heading not required.)

.... Witham Captain, R.E.
O.C. 3rd Field Squadron R.E.
May 1915 (9th sheet)

Instructions regarding War Diaries and Intelligence Summaries are contained in F.S. Regs., Part II. and the Staff Manual respectively. Title pages will be prepared in manuscript.

Hour, Date, Place	Summary of Events and Information	Remarks and references to Appendices
May 25.	Took over the information of 2 weeks continuing of Belgium on the line of trenches from MENIN GATE to canal junction making YPRES from 2nd Fd Sqdn R.E. Worked as above by day. Clearing fire around barricades, roads, within inclines open entrenchments, loopholes etc.	
26 – 27.	As above.	
28.		
29.	Heard that 3rd Cav. Div. had been coming up to relieve 2nd Cav. Div. of 7 had on above work on trenches at YPRES to Major Maclury OC b/1st Fd. Coy R.E. 3rd Fd Sqdn back in frances & Jarkrin had operating fr. 3rd Cav. Div. 3rd Cav. Div. occupying trenches from HOOGE in enemy from 1 – 24. b. inclusive to 1 – 24. b.	

Army Form C. 2118.

WAR DIARY
or
INTELLIGENCE SUMMARY

(Erase heading not required.)

Watson .... Captain, R.E.
O.C. 3rd Field Squadron R.E.

May 1915 (10ᵗʰ sheet)

Instructions regarding War Diaries and Intelligence Summaries are contained in F.S. Regs., Part II. and the Staff Manual respectively. Title pages will be prepared in manuscript.

Hour, Date, Place	Summary of Events and Information	Remarks and references to Appendices
May 30ᵗʰ	Both troops working N. of HOOGE village. Indians dug holes in houses facing North & working in front of them.	
31ˢᵗ	ditto. Constructing a trench on road N. of HOOGE village. Indians found loop holes only of village as front of the stables N. of the Chateau's unused front horizontally.	
June 1ˢᵗ	Col Watson CRE 3ʳᵈ Divⁿ took over general charge & instructed Capt Johnson 56ᵗʰ Fd Coy & Capt Wick him Fd Troop Saffron's troop to cooperate with me. Capt Saffron's troop had been instructed that HOOGE until 29ᵗʰ May VIIIᵗʰ ult. village was to be evacuated in the event of a heavy attack, but the orders were being on 29ᵗʰ May countermanded it with a strong hint for well-armed defence it to be held at all cost. Rations & ammunition for 48 hours being stored in the village & Garden surrounding it. The water in command of on the 30ᵗʰ 31ˢᵗ but was very RE were available until Col Watson came to our assistance.	(further report attached Appendix)

(73989) W4141—463. 400,000. 9/14. H.& J. Ltd. Forms/C. 2118/10.

Army Form C. 2118.

Captain T.E. [illegible]

WAR DIARY
or
INTELLIGENCE SUMMARY.
(Erase heading not required.)

O.C. 3rd Field Squadron R.E.

June 1915 [1st Sheet]

Hour, Date, Place	Summary of Events and Information	Remarks and references to Appendices
June 1st. 11·15 a.m.	In accordance with above general instructions the following work was arranged for nights of 1–2 June. (1) Field Troop Sotheron Munro to dig a section trench for 40 men the N.W. of Hooge village, on the east side of the line running from west end of Hooge village to west end of BELLEWAARDE LAKE. I saw the place, the Chateau & annexe & Chateau in good state of defence. Position was up road the fort. Owing to their late arrival, this work was not commenced till about midnight & the 3. D. Gs [the K. D. Gs. who had relieved the 3. D. Gs. at Hooge] apparently never held the position – consequently infantry front to the N.W. of the village. (2) The 3rd Troop Snelson worked on 200 M.E. woods & commenced a new second line trench through the middle of the wood, instead of along the edge.	Sketch Shewn. Ypres defences in front of & including Hooge attached. Sketch numbered June 1915 (1st Sheet B.)

Army Form C. 2118.

..V.L.Shaw...... Captain, R.E
O.C. 3rd Field Squadron R.E.

June 1915 (2 - Sheet)

WAR DIARY
or
INTELLIGENCE SUMMARY.
(Erase heading not required.)

Instructions regarding War Diaries and Intelligence Summaries are contained in F.S. Regs., Part II. and the Staff Manual respectively. Title pages will be prepared in manuscript.

Hour, Date, Place	Summary of Events and Information	Remarks and references to Appendices

June 1st Cont.

(2) The 56' Fd Co/RE started completion the wiring along the South & West of HOOGE village and adopted the existing trench to the Westerny South by digging T heads to the myriam directions.

June 2nd

Owing to the Germans having occupied the Chateau & annexe, & new suffocation bombs to N.W. of the village. He work at these points could not be completed.

Meanwhile the Early Troop Siskens Pknan occupied Hengelo in between "Kruyp-rest" trenches at West end of ZONNE WOOD.
56' Coy RE bivouaced MENIN road at West end of village
3rd Fd Sq RE dug a dry communication trench leading ground from N. end of ZONNE WOOD up to the HOOGE village.

Instructions regarding War Diaries and Intelligence Summaries are contained in F.S. Regs., Part II. and the Staff Manual respectively. Title pages will be prepared in manuscript.

WAR DIARY
or
INTELLIGENCE SUMMARY.
(Erase heading not required.)

W......... Captain, R.E
O.C. 3rd Field Squadron R.E.

Army Form C. 2118.

June 1915. (3: Sheet)

Hour, Date, Place	Summary of Events and Information	Remarks and references to Appendices
June 3.	Capt J.C. Witham R.E. OC Field Troop Sellar's Piney, worked whilst in Itooge ridge.	
	Indian RE not employed.	
	56 Coy RE worked in Itooge ridge, but as the Lincolns N.L. & 1 who had succeeded the K.O.G.C. failed to dislodge the Germans, the work could not be carried out.	
	3rd Fd Sqn RE informed the defences of the stable with sandbags & loopholes, cleared up heavy rifle fire. It was intended to just up an active & was continuously hand grenades.	

WAR DIARY
or
INTELLIGENCE SUMMARY.
(Erase heading not required.)

V.H.Sam .... Captain, R.E.
O.C. 3rd Field Squadron R.E.

June 1915. (4 Sheet)

Army Form C. 2118.

Hour, Date, Place	Summary of Events and Information	Remarks and references to Appendices
June 4th	Went to HOOGE certain by SE Ln RE, as infantry of III division had now taken them over that of the line. 3rd Fd Sqn. informed the "south" trench in J.13.C - J.19.a.1 behind the front where the Germans here still alleged to be mining. Orders here were to the troops there to hold front line strong & that balance of troops in "South" trench, in case 1 the Germans conducted any mines. I met Major Blake OC 1st Wilts + conducted him all round HOOGE, on the 1st Wilts relieved the Lincoln this night.	
June 5th	3rd Cav. Div. leaves trenches, & 3rd Fd Sqn returns to billets at RENESCURE.	

Army Form C. 2118.

.... Captain, R.E.
O.C. 3rd Field Squadron R.E.   June 1915. (5 sheets)

WAR DIARY
or
INTELLIGENCE SUMMARY.
(Erase heading not required.)

Instructions regarding War Diaries and Intelligence Summaries are contained in F.S. Regs., Part II. and the Staff Manual respectively. Title pages will be prepared in manuscript.

Hour, Date, Place	Summary of Events and Information	Remarks and references to Appendices
June 11.	Major C.E.P. Sankey joins 3rd Fd. Sqdn d assumes command.	
16.	2 Lieut Theodore Smith R.E. joined unit.	
June 1 –	General return to all units. Cleaning & sharpening tools. Painting wagons.	
June 15.	Cullehalle Foot explosant amount, with additions for Inman bridge.	

(73989) W4141—463. 400,000. 9/14. H.&J.Ltd. Forms/C. 2118/10.

War Diary
3rd Fd. Sqn RE.

Vitkin
CNPG

June 1915. 1st Sheet B.

xxxx wire entanglements
—— communication trenches
—— fire trenches
IIII communication trenches adjoining to fire trenches.

Reference ZILLEBEKE Sheet 1/10,000

Redoubt
Germans
Annexe Chateau
I.12.d
Stables — HOOGE Fort
J.13.a
From YPRES
I.18.a
Subterranean
Wet
Zouave Wood
I.18.c
Ivy
To MENIN
Wet
Ivy
J.13.d
I.18.d

From a sketch by Capt. V. H. Simon R.E. 3/6/15

121/0807

3rd Cavalry Division

3rd Field Squadron RE
Vol VIII
June to Sept. 15.

Kitchen... Captain. R.E.

WAR DIARY for O.C. 3rd Field Squadron R.E.
or
INTELLIGENCE SUMMARY.
(Erase heading not required.)

June 1915 [6th sheet] & July 1915 [6th sheet]

Army Form C. 2118.

Hour, Date, Place	Summary of Events and Information	Remarks and references to Appendices
June 6-30 / July 1-31	A third troop was formed during this period. The NCOs drawn from other 1 & 2 sections allotted as far as they went go. The necessary promotions and transfers were made on 5/7/15, & on 4/7/15 @ equipment of 13 July-trained sappers arrived for the Tate. During July the substructure for making cable ry & bridge in conjunction with the troop collapsible boat equipment arrived, & the troop was exercised in its use. Brigade classes have been held in the period, both instruction in demolitions with use of various kinds of hand grenades, beam, pier etc. The brigade practised crossing canals, trestle bridges, rafts made of squadron cooperators, junior & swimming parties with entire first time. Sapts. J & swimming rope have been practised.	

WAR DIARY
or
INTELLIGENCE SUMMARY.
(Erase heading not required.)

Army Form C. 2118.

W. Sham .... Captain, R.E.
for O.C. 3rd Field Squadron R.E.
July (2nd sheet)

Hour, Date, Place	Summary of Events and Information	Remarks and references to Appendices
July 1-31 (cont)	During July, digging parties from 3rd Cavalry division constructed a line of defence works from Hill 63, I.N.W. of PLOEGSTEERT WOOD] to a point east of NEUVE ÉGLISE. One troop of the Field Squadron went to supervise the work. Billets moved from RENESCURE to chateau of QUIESTÈDE about July 10th. On July 20th two troops of the Field Squadron & a digging party of about 900 men from the division proceeded to ELVERDINGHE and placed the village in a state of all-round defence. On August 9th the work, which was nearing completion, was handed over to 1st Cavalry Division.	

WAR DIARY for ~~Intelligence~~ L.H. Sim.........Captain. R.E
O.C 3rd Field Squadron R.E   Army Form C. 2118.

INTELLIGENCE SUMMARY.
(Erase heading not required.)

August 1915 [1st Sheet]

Instructions regarding War Diaries and Intelligence Summaries are contained in F.S. Regs., Part II. and the Staff Manual respectively. Title pages will be prepared in manuscript.

Hour, Date, Place	Summary of Events and Information	Remarks and references to Appendices
August 1915.	On August 9th the unit was moved from QUIESTÈDE to ERNY ST JULIEN.	
August 16 – Sept 4	VINCLY. The 3 troops is a digging party of 1960 men from the divisional headed to FREMENTIÈRES. Instructed defences on the north east, south & the town.	
20	Lieut DENNIS THEODORE-SMITH killed in action. He had been instructed in mounted duties.	12/8/15 Spr 34582 Ambrose wounded 14/8/15 Spr 72671 Vaughan wounded
27	Reinforcement of 43 sappers arrived. Consisting of 19 sappers and 1 Pte. ASC.	
14 – 30	Reinforcements arrived. 1 driver and 1 dismounted man from various RE units. Drafts of were trained in expectation	

(73989) W4141—463. 400,000. 9/14. H.&J.Ltd. Forms/C. 2118/10.

Army Form C. 2118.

WAR DIARY
or
INTELLIGENCE SUMMARY.
(Erase heading not required.)

for O.C. 3rd Field Squadron R.E. ......1/Lt Sturm........ Captain, R.E

September 1915 [1st sheet.]

Instructions regarding War Diaries and Intelligence Summaries are contained in F.S. Regs., Part II. and the Staff Manual respectively. Title pages will be prepared in manuscript.

Hour, Date, Place	Summary of Events and Information	Remarks and references to Appendices
September 5.	The unit at last has the (strength) of on this date the 4.5 troops was formed. He necessary promotion being made to complete establishment of N.C.Os. Troop & Squadron drill commenced on 6.7.15 recruits rides & lectures continuing.	
Fld 12	On completion of 11 months of Service in France. He Johnson is a Sapper in He casualties sustained. [original Strength of unit, 4 officers, 1 RAMC officer, about 120 other ranks.] Strength now 6 officers, 1 RAMC officer, about 200 other ranks.]	

(73989) W4141—463. 400,000. 9/14. H.&J.Ltd. Forms/C. 2118/10.

W. H. Shore ......Captain, R.E.
for O.C. 3rd Field Squadron R.E.   Army Form C. 2118.

WAR DIARY
or
INTELLIGENCE SUMMARY.
(Erase heading not required.)

September 1915. [2nd Sheet]

Hour, Date, Place	Summary of Events and Information	Remarks and references to Appendices
Sept 1915 (contd)	Summary of casualties for 11 months	

	Killed died of wounded evacuated sick
	                         wounds
	Officers 2 1 3 — 1
	Other ranks 3 2 6 9 35
	    Total 5 2 9 9 35	

	Percentage of average strength of 150. killed & wounded sick. Officers 100 % nil Other ranks 8 % 24 %.	
Sept 5.	2nd Lieut M. L. COBB joined unit.	

3 ga Agri R.R.
Sept to Dec Oct
Vol 9 to 13

War Diary of
3rd Fd Sqdn RE
September 1915 - Jan 1916
inclusive

[signature] C/RE
....
O.C. 3rd Field Squadron R.E.

22 2/16

Rec 25/2/16

Instructions regarding War Diaries and Intelligence Summaries are contained in F.S. Regs., Part II and the Staff Manual respectively. Title pages will be prepared in manuscript.

WAR DIARY
or
INTELLIGENCE SUMMARY
(Erase heading not required.)

Army Form C. 2118.

3rd Field Squadron R.E.
September 1915 (3rd Sheet)

Hour, Date, Place	Summary of Events and Information	Remarks and references to Appendices
Sept. 6 - 19. VINCLY	Troops & Squadron drill carried out & recruits taught equitation etc.	
Sept. 20.	2nd troop under Lieut. J. Ruggles detached from Squadron & attached to 7th Cav. Bde., & was not engaged in the attacks. Remainder of Squadron proceeded by route march to BOIS DES DAMES, near BRUAY, where we bivouacked in the woods, hidden from aeroplanes to some extent.	
22 - 24	The 3 troops were employed north by night, making Cavalry tracks so far as our front line trenches. These tracks were left clear of main roads & were brushed out with fuzze brands, & trenches & ditches from bridges over.	

(73989) W4141—463. 400,000. 9/14. H.&J.Ltd. Forms/C. 2118/10.

WAR DIARY 3rd Ph?? Squadron RE
INTELLIGENCE SUMMARY
(Erase heading not required.)

Army Form C. 2118.
September 1915. (4th Sheet)

Hour, Date, Place	Summary of Events and Information	Remarks and references to Appendices
Sept 25" PHILOSOPHE.	Moved with 3rd Cav Div to position of PHILOSOPHE. Southern VERMELLES, with a view to going through to PONT à VENDIN in the event of the infantry clearing a sufficient gap. During night 20·25 constructed 10 extra bridges, each on a wagon, on lot with ? etc for use ??. There were to be of use for the division through the gap. If the infantry of cavalry German trenches. The bridges were obtained from an Indian ammunition column.	
26" LOOS.	1st troop horsed OH with b? Cav Bde in the morning and assisted in consolidating the eastern outskirts of LOOS.	

WAR DIARY 3rd Field Squadron R.E.
or
INTELLIGENCE SUMMARY.

Schenke 1915 (5th Sheet.)

Army Form C. 2118.

Hour, Date, Place	Summary of Events and Information	Remarks and references to Appendices
Sept 27-29 LOOS.	The Squadron assisted the 6' & 8' Cavalry Brigades to dig trenches on the eastern outskirts of LOOS. Casualties: Lieut R D Park, slightly wounded. 1 Soffr. killed, 6 ORs wounded. Capt V H Seatt & Lieut R D Park received the DCM for their services at LOOS.	
Aug 28-29	Returned to Bois des DAMES, arriving 3/10/15 & bivouacked in the wood.	

WAR DIARY 3rd Field Squadron R.E.
INTELLIGENCE SUMMARY.
(Erase heading not required.)

Army Form C. 2118.

October 1915 (1st sheet)

Hour, Date, Place	Summary of Events and Information	Remarks and references to Appendices
Oct 3	Moved from Bois du DOUEE to huts in BURBURE	
Oct 18	Moved huts to huts at LUGY near PRUGES.	
Oct 20	Capt Simon detailed for operations (or work) under Engineer-in-chief on BCD line near SEMPY. One Subaltern (Lieut Cobb, then Lieut Ruggard, then Lieut Jones) with 65 Labour Battalion on BCD line near PRUGES.	
Nov 17	Moved to huts in COUDELLE NEUVE	
3	Lieut L.E. Trevor posted to RE Training Centre in England	
18	Temp 2 Lt R F Jones joined Squadron	
Oct – Dec	Nothing worth troubling etc for the division on & writing in improving Horse Standings & Horse Shelters.	

Nov + Dec. 1915
Jan - 1916

3rd Field Squadron R.E.

3rd Fd. Sqdn. R.E. Army Form C. 2118.
Vols. 11-13
Nov 1915. Dec 1915. Jan 1916.

WAR DIARY
or
INTELLIGENCE SUMMARY.
(Erase heading not required.)

Instructions regarding War Diaries and Intelligence Summaries are contained in F.S. Regs., Part II. and the Staff Manual respectively. Title pages will be prepared in manuscript.

Hour, Date, Place	Summary of Events and Information	Remarks and references to Appendices
Nov 1st /	Digging trenches from the Brewery sent to SERCUS & watering place trig Christmas.	
Dec. 25.12.15	Lieut J. Fryzell attached ADC to C.G.S. at GHQ	
Jan 1916. 1st	a troop & strength 30 (Horses) 61 - ORs } proceeding with cavalry div mounted division to trenches east of VERMELLES.	
1.1.16	2nd Lieut G T BRISTED joined	
20:	2nd Lt E.F CHAPPELL joined	
22	Lieut R D PINK wounded	
31	2nd Lieut G.H. BICKEL joined.	

OC 3rd Field Squadron R.E.

(73989) W4141—463. 400,000. 9/14. H.&J.Ltd. Forms/C. 2118/10.

Army Form C. 2118.

WAR DIARY
or
INTELLIGENCE SUMMARY. J H Ian Clarke
O.C. 3rd Field Squadron R.E.
(Erase heading not required.)

Instructions regarding War Diaries and Intelligence Summaries are contained in F.S. Regs., Part II. and the Staff Manual respectively. Title pages will be prepared in manuscript.

Hour, Date, Place	Summary of Events and Information	Remarks and references to Appendices
Jan 31st 1916	19780 2/Cpl HENDERSON killed in action.	
Feb 3rd	Temp Lt E.F. CHAPPELL killed in action.	
	14573 2/Cpl G.W. MATTHESON wounded.	
7	33105 Sapper TINSLEY wounded	
8	2/Lt G.I. EATON - MATTHEWS joined	
12	The Troop with the Dismounted Cavalry Division returned to COUPELLE NEUVE.	
	Troop Leaders. 1st 2/Lt Mathew	
	2nd 2/Lt Braster	
	3rd 2/Lt Cobb	
	4th 2/Lt Tower.	
15-24	The Troop did dismounted drill and rifle exercises, and were lectured on Map Reading and demolition.	
24-28th	Practice in using trapping knife.	

Army Form C. 2118.

WAR DIARY
or
INTELLIGENCE SUMMARY.
(Erase heading not required.)

Lt. Van WARE
O.C. 3rd Field Squadron R.E.

Instructions regarding War Diaries and Intelligence Summaries are contained in F.S. Regs., Part II. and the Staff Manual respectively. Title pages will be prepared in manuscript.

Hour, Date, Place	Summary of Events and Information	Remarks and references to Appendices
March.	Training in mounted Drill, Rifling Equipment. Lectures on the Care of Horses. Packing Tool Carts.	
3rd	Temp. N. at Pollock Tunnel.	
April.	Trestle Bridging and Use of Spars. Drill in R. Ration gas masks. Solutions and a scheme on the Defence of locality. N.C.O.'s did a report on a Demolition scheme and the materials available locally for bridging. Route Marches.	
May 1st	Lt. J. Kiggell rejoined the Squadron from G.H.Q	

(73989) W4141—463. 400,000. 9/14. H.&J.Ltd. Forms/C. 2118/10.

WAR DIARY or **INTELLIGENCE SUMMARY**.

Army Form C. 2118.

3rd Field Squadron R.E.

MARCH 1918.

Hour, Date, Place	Summary of Events and Information	Remarks and references to Appendices
May 1916. May 1st–15th.	Trestle bridging and use of spars; Rafting. Trial of bridge for Sappers.	WAR 16711
May 15th	Squadron less 1st & 2nd Troops, moved to camp at Tinqueut, for further training in bridging, summer horses, overhead cables, etc.	
	1st & 2nd Troops moved to training area at St Riquier with Divion, having crowds of experiments in carrying him material for mounted Sappers.	
May 21st	1st & 2nd Troops joined remainder of Squadron at Tinqueut camp.	
[illegible]	Remainder of Squadron moved from camp to Hronien.	
June 1st	higher bridge	
June 3rd		31371 L/Cpl. E Coldman awarded McMillan Medal

WAR DIARY
or
INTELLIGENCE SUMMARY.
(Erase heading not required.)

Army Form C. 2118.

War Diary of R.E. 3rd Field Squadron

3rd FIELD SQUADRON, R.E.

Hour, Date, Place	Summary of Events and Information	Remarks and references to Appendices
June 4th	Squadron less bridging train left La Tryport, for Enguille Neuve.	
June 7th	Bridging train joined Squadron at COUPELLE NEUVE.	
June 10th	Carried out experiments in filling in & hindering means of guerilla & improvised.	
June 16-20th	Worked on line Nure & Fruges, making M.G. Emplacements and dug outs.	June 17th Temp Lieut M. CoBB. and 17/29 2nd Cpl. act. S/Batchelor returned to depot etc.? from dispatches.
June 21st–23rd	Repair of panels & ladders all ranges etc.	
June 24th	Marched by night to Estrées les Crecy arriving morning 25th.	
June 25th	Marched by night to La HAIE F.me. (N. of DOMARTEN-PONTHIEU) arriving morning 26th.	

Army Form C. 2118.

3rd
FIELD SQUADRON.
R.E.

WAR DIARY
or
INTELLIGENCE SUMMARY.
(Erase heading not required.)

Instructions regarding War Diaries and Intelligence Summaries are contained in F.S. Regs., Part II. and the Staff Manual respectively. Title pages will be prepared in manuscript.

Hour, Date, Place	Summary of Events and Information	Remarks and references to Appendices
June 26th	Moved to concentration area NE of La Neuville. 1st, 2nd, 3rd Troops went in advance to cut gaps in wire entanglements W. of ALBERT.	
June 27th	Troops continued to cut further gaps in wire entanglements.	
June 28th to 30th July 1st	Confined to camp owing to orders.	

3rd Cav Div

Army Form C. 2118.

WAR DIARY
or
INTELLIGENCE SUMMARY.
(Erase heading not required.)

hr cork ERS.
O.C. 3rd Field Squadron R.E.

Vol 19

3rd
FIELD SQUADRON
R.E.
Date. 8.8.16

Instructions regarding War Diaries and Intelligence Summaries are contained in F.S. Regs., Part II. and the Staff Manual respectively. Title pages will be prepared in manuscript.

Hour, Date, Place	Summary of Events and Information	Remarks and references to Appendices
July 1st & 2nd	Awaited orders in camp at BONNAY.	
July 3rd.	Left BONNAY and marched to HOCQUINCOURT.	
July 4th-6th	Fatigues in camp at HOCQUINCOURT.	
July 7th	Standing bye at 12 hours notice.	
July 8th	Left camp at HOCQUINCOURT and marched to a new camping ground at VECQUEMONT on the SOMME.	
July 9th & 10th	Fatigues in camp.	
July 11th	Four troops under Lieuts C A Pollock G J EATON-MATTHEWS made cavalry tracks running EAST from Le CARCAILLOT FARM S of MEAULTE to CAFFET WOOD, S of CARNOY.	

(73989) W4141—463. 400,000. 9/14. H.&J.Ltd. Forms/C. 2118/10.

Army Form C. 2118.

3rd F.E.

W Ch
for O.C. 3rd Field Squadron R.E.

[stamp: 3rd FIELD SQUADRON R.E. 8.8.16]

WAR DIARY
or
INTELLIGENCE SUMMARY.
(Erase heading not required.)

Instructions regarding War Diaries and Intelligence Summaries are contained in F.S. Regs., Part II. and the Staff Manual respectively. Title pages will be prepared in manuscript.

Hour, Date, Place	Summary of Events and Information	Remarks and references to Appendices
July 12th & 13th & 14th	Lieut. R.F. Jones with 30 Sappers + 5 G.S. wagons VECQUEMONT - to erect five 9000 gallon water troughs in CARNOY VALLEY at Le TAILUS-BOISÉ. This officer & ** all the other ranks bivouacked for night at DERNACOURT. Remainder await further orders at VECQUEMONT.	
July 15th	Lieut R.F. Jones + party rejoined Squadron at VECQUEMONT.	
July 16th & 17th	Remained at camp awaiting orders.	
July 18th	Lieuts M. COBB & G. BRISTED and 50 Sappers left VECQUEMONT & proceeded to BLACKWOOD, E. of ALBERT. 15 sappers were running from ALBERT eastwards to BECOURT.	
July 19th & 20th	Work was continued	

Army Form C. 2118.

WAR DIARY
or
INTELLIGENCE SUMMARY.
(Erase heading not required.)

W.L.Cahill Lt.G
for O.C. 3rd Field Squadron R.E.

Hour, Date, Place	Summary of Events and Information	Remarks and references to Appendices
July 21st.	Lieuts M L COBB + G BRISTED + party slightly wounded in forward road making between BECOURT + FRICOURT.	
July 22, 23, 24	Continued forward road.	
July 25th.	Squadron mtr transport & 1 man to Third hours left VECQUEMONT for camp at BECOURT, for work with dismounted parting cavalry on trenches to front of CONTALMAISON + in MAMETZ wood.	Lieut C A POLLOCK wounded. 25 P 31. Dr Proudfoot J. Recruited 55220 Dr WHEELDON J wounded
July 26th	Lieut BRISTED arrive at VECQUEMONT. for BECOURT to replace Lieut C A POLLOCK. Work in trenches continued	
July 27th 28th 29th 30th	Work in trenches continued.	July 28th. Lieut J Russell reports G.S.W. Du p's midfinger. July 29th Fin knee wounded. "Lieut. R A HAY Jones. July 30th. 25351 Dr NOBLE W C wounded.
July 31st.	Squadron returned from BECOURT to VECQUEMONT.	

August 1916 — 3 Fd Sqd R.E.

WAR DIARY / INTELLIGENCE SUMMARY

Army Form C. 2118.

O.C. 3rd Field Squadron R.E.

Hour, Date, Place	Summary of Events and Information	Remarks and references to Appendices
Aug. 1st	Squadron moved from Vecquemont to Le Quesnoy.	
Aug 2nd	Lieut BRISTED and 22 other ranks left Le Quesnoy to work in LEIPSIG Redoubt with 7" Coy Bedf. M. Gunners. Work consisted of making M.G. emplacements & shelters.	
	Remainder of Squadron left Le Quesnoy for ONEUX.	
Aug 4th	Squadron moved from ONEUX to DOMPIERRE.	
5th	Squadron moved from DOMPIERRE to TORCY.	
Aug 9th	Lieut Mc CABB & Lieut HAY and 50 O.Rs. left TORCY for AVELUY to make OPs for II CORPS. OPs — LEIPSIG REDOUBT & W. OVILLERS	Lieut Mc CABB handed in AVELUY
Aug 13	Lieut JONES. & relief left TORCY to relieve Lt Bristed, & carried on work LEIPSIG REDOUBT.	
Aug 16	MACONOCHIE joined	

2/Lieut

Army Form C. 2118.

August 1916

WAR DIARY
INTELLIGENCE SUMMARY
(Erase heading not required.)

O.C. 3rd Field Squadron R.E.

Hour, Date, Place	Summary of Events and Information	Remarks and references to Appendices
Aug. 15th		T/Lieut. HAY. wounded.
21st		Lieut. H. GUTTERIDGE joined
Aug 23		L/Cpl HOOK wounded
Aug 25th	T/Lieut MACONACHIE'S party formed at 3rd Cav Div HQ. party at BOUZINCOURT.	
	T/Lieut EATON-MATTHEWS. Relieved Lt JONES at South Bluffs N of AVELUY	
Aug 26th	15 Sappers relieved some of Sappers under T/Lt EATON-MATTHEWS T/LIEUT MACONACHIE and 2/Lt EATON-MATTHEWS att to parties to Capt. SIMON at AVELUY.	
26-30th	T/Lt EATON MATTHEWS W/S and 30 sappers working on O.R. Dugouts for Gunners of II CORPS. 2/Lt MACONACHIE working with Cav Div HQ party on Cav Div HQ party.	
31st	T/Lt EATON-MATTHEWS working with Cav Div HQ party.	

Army Form C 2118.

Vol 2 J
September
O.C. 3rd Field Squadron R.E.

WAR DIARY
INTELLIGENCE SUMMARY
(Erase heading not required.)

Instructions regarding War Diaries and Intelligence Summaries are contained in F. S. Regs., Part II. and the Staff Manual respectively. Title pages will be prepared in manuscript.

Hour, Date, Place	Summary of Events and Information	Remarks and references to Appendices
Sept 1st	Work continued with Cav. Digging Party.	Capt V H Simon M.C. wounded but remained at duty
Sept 2nd	—	
Sept 5th	Lieuts - Gutteridge - Jones + Bristed, and 10 other ranks left Tracy for Aveluy to relieve previous party	
Sept 6th	Lieuts Eaton-Matthews Maconachie and 10 other ranks returned from working with 4th/7th party, to Torcy.	
Sept 7th	Lieuts Gutteridge - Jones - Bristed and remainder of sappers rejoined squadron at Torcy.	
Sept 10th	Squadron left Torcy for Dompierre	
11th	Squadron left Dompierre for Conteville	
12th	Squadron left Conteville for Belloy-sur-Somme	
13th	Remained at Belloy-sur-Somme	

WAR DIARY
INTELLIGENCE SUMMARY

(Erase heading not required.)

Army Form C. 2118.

September

No. C.174778

3rd Field Squadron R.E.

For O.C. 3rd Field Squadron R.E.

Hour, Date, Place	Summary of Events and Information	Remarks and references to Appendices
Sept 14th	Squadron left BELLOY-SUR-SOMME for DAOURS.	
15th	('A' Echelon) Squadron less 'B' Echelon left DAOURS for LA NEUVILLE	'B' Echelon comprises 1 G.S. wagon, 1 6 Boat wagon, Cooks cart + baggage wagon + dismounted sappers.
	'B' Echelon remains at DAOURS. 22 Sappers joined Squadron.	
Sept 17th	'A' Echelon of Squadron left LA NEUVILLE + rejoined 'B' Echelon at DAOURS.	
Sept 18th–22nd	Remained at DAOURS.	
Sept 22nd	Squadron left DAOURS for Le GARD.	
23rd	Squadron left Le GARD for FROHEN-LE-GRAND.	
24th	Squadron left FROHEN-LE-GRAND for camp ½ mile S.E. of DOURIEZ.	

WAR DIARY
INTELLIGENCE SUMMARY

September 1914

Army Form C. 2118.

W.L. Cath Lt RE

O.C. 3rd Field Company

Hour, Date, Place	Summary of Events and Information	Remarks and references to Appendices
Sept 25 - 30th	Squadron remained in camp ½ mile S.E. of DOURIEZ.	Sept. 29 1 NCO + 10 Sappers joined squadron.
Sept 30th	Squadron left camp ½ mile S.E. of DOURIEZ for SAULCHOY.	

Army Form C. 2118.

WAR DIARY
or
INTELLIGENCE SUMMARY.
(Erase heading not required.)

October 1916

O.C. 3rd Field Squadron R.E.

Remarks and references to Appendices: Vol 22

Hour, Date, Place	Summary of Events and Information
Oct 1-3	Arranging billets at SAULCHOY and riding drill for new Sappers.
4th	Squadron left SAULCHOY for FROHEN-le-GRAND
5th	Squadron left FROHEN-le-GRAND for camp near COLIN.
7.	Commenced two water supplies. (1) 3 Troops erects two tanks 9000 gallons each – and fitted up 20 canvas water troughs, *horse-troughs [crossed out]* at COURCELLES au BOIS Sheet 57D J 23 d 7.3. (2) 1 Troop erects 10 canvas watertroughs and stand pumps at COIGNEUX Sheet 57D. J. 8 a 5.2.
8-12 a.	Continued the two water supplies & finished them on 12th Oct.
13th	Staff 2 Troops started making 12 light-antitank bridges. 1 Troop started an observation post covered by steel shelter. Let into ground at K 21 Central Sheet 57D. 1 Troop cleaned watersupply at St Leger cavalry β 1-9000 gallon tank and 10 canvas troughs at I 11 d 60. Sheet 57D and erected of Merryweath pump at I 11 d 5.3 Sheet 57D.

Army Form C. 2118.

WAR DIARY
or
INTELLIGENCE SUMMARY.
(Erase heading not required.)

October 1916

for. M.C.th 2/1/05
O.C. 37th Field Squadron R.E.

Hour, Date, Place	Summary of Events and Information	Remarks and references to Appendices
14th–19th.	Continued above works – completion 19th – including the making of 6 Heavy Water for Motor Machine Gun Corps. (Heavy Battery)	
20th.	Started working for XIII Corps. Erection of water supply between COUIN & St LÉGER consisting of Pipe line 4" from Smart Honeycastle pump at COUIN to the creeks. 1 tank 5000 gallon at J.1.c.82 and one from tank to 14 wooden troughs to be erected at J.1.c.71 Sheet 57D.	
	Continued & completed above works except of placing wood troughs –	
	1 Trough extension completed. Placing wood troughs	
20–31.	Continued and completed above works.	

WAR DIARY or INTELLIGENCE SUMMARY

Army Form C. 2118.

November 1916   Hd. C.M. bapte
for O.C. 3rd Field Squadron R.E.

Hour, Date, Place	Summary of Events and Information	Remarks and references to Appendices
1st – 2nd	Water supply for XIII Corps at COUIN	Vol 2
3rd	Moved from COUIN to FROHEN LE GRAND	
4th	Moved from FROHEN LE GRAND to SAULCHOY	
5th	Moved from SAULCHOY to LE PUITS BERRAULT (2 kilometres S of WAILLY). Lt Bristed and 22 ORs left Le Puits-Berrault to erect shelters + improve under billets for 7th Cav Bde.	
7th	Lt Maconachie + 22 ORs left Le Puits-Berrault to erect shelters + improve under billets for 8th Cav Bde.	
	II Lt Jones + 28 ORs left Le Puits-Berrault for work at sawmills at MONTREUIL.	
	Lt Gutteridge + 2Lt Eaton-Matthews working for 8th Cav Bde + 40 ORs + Dw: School, in improving under billets + erecting stables.	
19th – 30th	Lt Bristed + 180 ORs left Le Puits Berrault for work with 7th Cav Pioneer Bn under II Corps. Camped at RAFFIR camp – W. edge of AVELUY WOOD – work consisted of

Army Form C. 2118.

WAR DIARY
or
INTELLIGENCE SUMMARY.
(Erase heading not required.)

hc AB Capn 128
for O.C 3rd Field Squadron hh

Hour, Date, Place	Summary of Events and Information	Remarks and references to Appendices
19-30 (contd).	Repairs road from HAMEL to BEAUCOURT. 2/Lieut EATON-MATTEWS and 180 O.Rs left for PUITS BERRAULT with 8th Cav. Pioneer Btn for work under V Corps, billets at P.18 Central Sheet 57D), work consisted of road-making; and digging support line between BEAUMONT-HAMEL & BAUCOURT. Work by day and night 24/25). Later whole Batt Btn on road making. Three Company on road between ACHEUX. One Company repairing road near ENGLEBELMER—HAMEL Remainder of Squadron work as before erecting stables, improving water billets for divisions	

3rd Field Sqn R.E.

WAR DIARY
or
INTELLIGENCE SUMMARY.
(Erase heading not required.)

Army Form C. 2118.

December 1916

M.A.Cooper R.E.

Hour, Date, Place	Summary of Events and Information	Remarks and references to Appendices
Dec 1st – 15th	Lt Bristol and 18 ORs working with 9th Cav Pioneer Bn under II Corps – work consisted of improving road from HAMEL to BEAUCOURT.	
	2nd Lieut EATON-MATTHEWS + 18 ORs left working with 9th Cav Pioneer B.E. under XIII Corps – work consisted of improving roads at ACHEUX & ENGLEBELMER-HAMEL road.	
	Remainder of Squadron working at improving shelters, billets & erecting stables for the division.	
Dec 15th – 21st	2nd Lieut EATON-MATTHEWS and party with a machine gun employed in taking parts – improving existing trench near BEAUMONT-HAMEL.	15th L/cpl Mathieu wounded
Sarton Dec 15th – 21st	Lt Bristol & party working on roads & bridges under IV Corps.	

(73989) W4141–463. 400,000. 9/14. H.&J.Ltd. Forms/C. 2118/10.

WAR DIARY or INTELLIGENCE SUMMARY.

(Erase heading not required.)

Army Form C. 2118.

M.G.M. Corps

Hour, Date, Place	Summary of Events and Information	Remarks and references to Appendices
Dec 20th	Lt Gutteridge & 20 ORs leave Le Puits-Berrault to relieve	
21st	2/Lt Eaton-Matthews & party. Brook Wtr 6 h. Rouen Rd.	4/2/17
	2/Lt Eaton-Matthews & party return to Le Puits-Berrault.	
Dec 23rd	RAGGe II Lieut Maconachie & 8 ORs leave Le Puits Berrault	
	Relieve 2/Lt Bristed & 8 ORs - Brinkum 7 h. Rouen Rd.	
24th	Lieut Bristed & 8 ORs return from work with 2/Lt Pierce B.C.	
Dec 28th	Remainder of Squadron continued work for improvement	Sgt Wright wounded
29th	of hutts & stables & drainage.	Cpl Finch wounded.

Army Form C. 2118.

WAR DIARY
or
INTELLIGENCE SUMMARY.
(Erase heading not required.)

Instructions regarding War Diaries and Intelligence Summaries are contained in F.S. Regs., Part II. and the Staff Manual respectively. Title pages will be prepared in manuscript.

3rd FIELD SQUADRON R.E.
FEB 10 1917

Hour, Date, Place	Summary of Events and Information	Remarks and references to Appendices
Jan 1st – 13th	Lieut. GUTTERIDGE & 20 ORs working with 6th Cav Pioneer Bn under XIII Corps – Work consisted of making dugouts & Lieut. MACONOCHIE & 16 ORs working with 7th Cav Pioneer Bn under V Corps – Work consisted of making truck and grass between THIEPVAL & BEAUMONT HAMEL. Lieut. JONES & 19 ORs under a Sapper at Savernake MONTREUIL making shelters for improvements of billets & horse lip.	
Jan 8th	Capt. COBB left Squadron Headquarters for course of instruction at Brigade School ARRAS.	
Jan 13th 21st	Lieut. JONES & 15 ORs working at Sawmills MONTREUIL. Lieut GUTTERIDGE & Lieut MACONOCHIE & 47 ORs working with 6th & 7th Cav Pioneer Bns under XIII Corps – working on railway BOULLENS – ARRAS.	

Army Form C. 2118.

WAR DIARY
or
INTELLIGENCE SUMMARY.
(Erase heading not required.)

January 1917. W.M.Adams

Instructions regarding War Diaries and Intelligence Summaries are contained in F.S. Regs., Part II. and the Staff Manual respectively. Title pages will be prepared in manuscript.

3rd FIELD SQUADRON, R.E.
FEB 10 1917

Hour, Date, Place	Summary of Events and Information	Remarks and references to Appendices
Jan 21st	Major V. H. Simon left Squadron Headquarters for course of instruction at R.E. School of Instruction G.H.Q. Troops at Le Parc near Houdin	
Jan 22 - 29th	Lieut Jones + 20 ORs not at Saumur to Montreuil + had days Montreuil	
	Lieut Gutteridge & Lieut Maconochie working with 6th & 7th Can Pionier Bn under XIII Corps - Instruments + Excavating Cutting at Doullens - Montricourt seeking Railway & railway between Doullens & Arras	
Jan 31st	Lieut Gutteridge + 200 ORs returned from work with 6th Can Pionier party to Squadron headquarters at Le Puits - Berrault	

WAR DIARY or INTELLIGENCE SUMMARY

3rd Army FIELD SQUADRON R.E.
No. 2 27/92

3 Yr Sqn RE
FEBRUARY 1917

Place	Date	Hour	Summary of Events and Information	Remarks and references to Appendices
	Feb 1 4:00 p.c.		Lieut MACONOCHIE & 16 ORs rejoined squadron at LE PUITS-BERAULT from working with 7th Cavalry Pioneer Battalion.	
			Lieuts Jones & 200 ORs under his orders rode to MONTRELOIS.	
			Remainder of Squadron Started Squadron Training	
Feb 5th to Feb 16th		8:45–9:15	Squadron Training — Run & Physical drill	
		9:30–1:45	Riding — Cav Training §§ 63–67, 69, 81, 84	
		2:00–2:30 p	Football Cav Training §§ 15–28	
		2:30–3:30 p	Lectures Knotting Lashings Hitches	
		3:0–4:00 p	Knotting & Lashing M.F.E §§ 69–73	
		6:15–6:45	Lecture on Training (Feb 5) — Haphazardry (Feb 5 & 6)	
	7th	8:45–9:15	Run & Physical drill	
		9:30–11:30	Riding — Cav Training §§ 63–67, 69, 80, 81	
			Handling [illegible]	
		2:30–3:30	Stables and Grooming [illegible]	
		4:30	Use of Spur M.F.E §§ 74–77	
		6:15–7:15	Lecture (Officers & NCOs) R.S reconnaissance in the advance	

3rd FIELD SQUADRON.
Army Form C. 2118.

WAR DIARY
or
INTELLIGENCE SUMMARY.

(Erase heading not required.)

February 1917.

Instructions regarding War Diaries and Intelligence Summaries are contained in F. S. Regs., Part II. and the Staff Manual respectively. Title pages will be prepared in manuscript.

Place	Date	Hour	Summary of Events and Information	Remarks and references to Appendices
	Feb 8	9.45–4.45	Squadron Train. Run & Physical drill	
	Feb 9	9.30–11.30	Squadron Train. Riding & Cav Train §§ 63-67, 69, 80, 81. Including Bayonets	
		2.0–2.30	Handling & arms Cav Train § 40-45	
		2.30–3.0	Lecture use of pan	
		3.0–4.0	Use of pans MFE 74-77	
		8.15–9.15	Lecture (Officers + NCO) Feb 9th Defence of localities	
	Feb 10	8.45–9.45	Scheme for Defence of localities.	Demolitions in Demolitions
		9.00–1.30	Run & Physical drill	
	Feb 12 & 13	8.45–9.15	Riding – Troop drill Cav Training §§ 115–128	
		9.30–11.30	Preliminary musketry	
		2.0–2.30	Lecture on Demolitions	
		2.30–3.0	"	
		3.0–4.0	Demolition Firing Charges MFE §§ 98–112.	
		4.15–6.45	Lecture Officers + NCO. Feb 13th Demolitions & testing of circuits	
			Feb 13th Maps reading	
	Feb 14	9.45–9.15	Run & Physical drill	
		9.30–11.30	Riding drill Cav Training §§ 115–128	

FIELD SQUADRON
Army Form C. 2118.

WAR DIARY
or
INTELLIGENCE SUMMARY.
(Erase heading not required.)

February 1917

Instructions regarding War Diaries and Intelligence Summaries are contained in F. S. Regs., Part II. and the Staff Manual respectively. Title pages will be prepared in manuscript.

Place	Date	Hour	Summary of Events and Information	Remarks and references to Appendices
	Feb 15th /16th	8.45-9.15	Squad training Run & Physical drill	
		9.30-11.20	Run Riding & Gas Training §119-128	
		2.0-2.30	Pulmonary Musketry	
		2.30-3.0	Lecture Demolition without Explosives	
		3.0-4.0	Demolition First charges & testing circuits	
	17th	8.45-11.30	Scheme Demolition	
	Feb 19th Mon	8.45-9.15	Run & Physical drill	
		9.30-11.30	Troop drill	
		2.0-3.0	Lecture Staff Management	
		3.0		
	Feb 21	8.45-11.30	Packing Tortoises Scheme Defence of bridges	
	Feb 22 /23rd	8.45-9.15	Run & Physical drill	
		9.30-11.30	Troop drill	
		2.0-3.0	Lecture Staff Management	
		3.0-4.0	Packing Packhorses	

Army Form C. 2118.

3rd FIELD SQUADRON R.E.

February. M.A. Earths

WAR DIARY
or
INTELLIGENCE SUMMARY.
(Erase heading not required.)

Place	Date	Hour	Summary of Events and Information	Remarks and references to Appendices
	Feb. 24th	9.45-1/30	Squadron Training	
	26 } 27 }	8.45-9.15	Scheme Defence of Locations. Run & Physical drill	
	3	9.30-1/30 2-4p	Troop drill & Musketry. Wiring drill.	

WAR DIARY or INTELLIGENCE SUMMARY

(Erase heading not required.)

Army Form C. 2118.

3 Fd Squad

MARCH 1917

Place	Date	Hour	Summary of Events and Information	Remarks and references to Appendices
	1/3/17		Lieut JONES & 28 ORs regin Squadron at Le PUITS-BERRAULT for Cavalry at MONTREUIL.	
	2/3/17		Lieut MACONOCHIE & 22 ORs left Le PUITS-BERRAULT for work under VII Corps, work consisted of erecting Radio hoops with neighbourhood of GOUY-EN-ARTOIS.	
	7/3/17		1 NCO & 3 ORs left Le PUITS-BERRAULT to repair cables at COUPELLE-NEUVE	
	9/3/17		1 NCO & 8 ORs regin unit from COUPELLE-NEUVE.	
	19/3/17		Lieut MACONOCHIE & 16 ORs regin unit at Le PUITS-BERRAULT from GOUY.	
	20/3/17		4 ORs regin unit from GOUY.	
	23/3/17		Lt RATTRAY & 10 ORs proceed to ARRAS from Le PUITS BERRAULT, and are attached to 3rd Cav Dismounted Batt for work under 14th Division, for the purpose of making a track for the cavalry through the British trenches.	
	27/3/17		Lieut JONES & 20 ORs left Le PUITS-BERRAULT to join Lieut RATTRAY & party at ARRAS	
			Remainder of Squadron continued to train during this month.	

Wh OH Copps
3 Field Squad RE

WAR DIARY or INTELLIGENCE SUMMARY

3rd Field Squadron

April 1917

Army Form C. 2118.

Place	Date	Hour	Summary of Events and Information	Remarks and references to Appendices
	1-7		+39 ORs	
	5th		Lieut RATT-KERR + Lieut JONES working under VII Corps on track for Cavalry. Squadron less Lieuts RATT-KERR & JONES & 35 ORs left LE PUITS-BERRAULT for MARIEUX.	
	7th		Squadron less party with VII Corps left MARIEUX for CONCHY in CANCHE "B" Echelon.	Lieut RATT-KERR wounded 6th.
	8th		Squadron less party with VII Corps left CONCHY en CANCHE for GOUY en ARTOIS - "B" Echelon moved to BUIRE-sur-CANCHE under OC ASC.	Sapper White wounded.
	9th		1st Troop under Lieut EATON-MATTHEWS joined 6th Bde, 8th Sqn + proceeded with 6th Bde. IInd Troop under Lieut BEISTED JONES joined 7th Bde & proceeded with it. IIIrd Troop under Lieut MACONOCHIE joined 8th Bde & proceeded with it. Remainder of Squadron followed on the 6th Bde under Capt COBB. Major SIMON JONES Durward Headquarters.	
	10th		VIII Troop under Lieut MACONOCHIE with 8th Bde the leading Bde moved to field inside W7 ARRAS where it remained several hours. This returned & bivouacs near TILLOY. From here the Bde proceeded to ORANGE HILL. The Bde then bivouaced for night GOD⁺ LACK junction WN FEUCHY road. I Troop under Lieut EATON-MATTHEWS accompanied 6th Bde & took position 8th Bde.	

Army Form C. 2118.

WAR DIARY
or
INTELLIGENCE SUMMARY.
(Erase heading not required.)

Place	Date	Hour	Summary of Events and Information	Remarks and references to Appendices
		10.°	II Troop under Lieut BRISTED accompanied 1st Bde, the reserve Bde. Remainder of Squadron under Capt COBB formed 2 echelon.	
		11.°	III Troop under Lieut MACONOCHIE proceeded in rear of RHG third MONCHY. RHG hy reserve regiment P/R Bde. Troop who this shelled in charge of remainder of Bde his checks retiring prior W. of FEUCHY road. Other troops accompanying the Bdes. Squadron met all troops returning to GOUY en ARTOIS.	
			Squadron moved from GOUY's ARTOIS to BEUCHE 2 miles SW of AUXI-le-CHATEAU.	
		14.°	Lieut JONES + 2 ORs rejoined from VII Corps.	
		16.°		
		18.°	Squadron proceeded to WADICOURT.	
		19.°	Trains at WADICOURT.	
		19-30	Lieut WHEATLEY joined from BASE.	

W McCarthy

WAR DIARY
or
INTELLIGENCE SUMMARY.
(Erase heading not required.)

Army Form C. 2118.

Place	Date	Hour	Summary of Events and Information	Remarks and references to Appendices
	May 3rd	9ᵃ	Bridging practice with attd boat equipment at VITZ-VILLEROY.	
		9ᵃ	Squadron leave WADICOURT for BEAUMETZ - W WHEATLEY + 70 ORs from reinforcement camp at FREVENT	
	10ᵗʰ		Squadron leave BEAUMETZ for VILLERS-BOCAGE -	
	11ᵗʰ		Squadron leave VILLERS-BOCAGE for MÉAULT.	
	12		Squadron leave MÉAULTE for BUIRE	
	14ᵗʰ		Start watchposts for 3 Cav Division coming into area. Each Brigade	
			+ troop circles of each Brigade + Divisional troops at the following points	
			6ᵗʰ Bde. J 28 d 3.9.	
			7ᵗʰ Bde I 29 a 3.7	
			8ᵗʰ Bde J 33 c 5.8. } Sheet 62c.	
			Div Troops J 33 b.22.	
			Amm Column J 23 d 7.7.	
	15ᵗʰ		Lieut WHEATLEY + 36 ORs join Squadron at BUIRE from reinforcement camp FREVENT	
	18ᵗʰ		Lieuts BRISTED - JARVIS - MACONOCHIE - EATON-MATTHEWS - WHEATLEY + 105 ORs left BUIRE for camp at E 12 b- 5.5. Sheet 62c.	

Army Form C. 2118.

WAR DIARY
or
INTELLIGENCE SUMMARY.
(Erase heading not required.)

Instructions regarding War Diaries and Intelligence Summaries are contained in F.S. Regs., Part II and the Staff Manual respectively. Title pages will be prepared in manuscript.

3rd FIELD SQUADRON R.E.
MAY 1917

Place	Date	Hour	Summary of Events and Information	Remarks and references to Appendices
	16 (Contd)		Major V. H. Simson + Capt. Corser join HQ of 2nd Cav Div at K.11.a.10.9. Sheet 62c from them 2nd Cav Div in outpost-line + Greenline, Lieut Brooks + party undertaking care 2nd Cav Div – Major V H Simon in charge of reconnaissance support in this area – Capt Corser in charge of Sir. Our group at ST EMILIE	
	25th		Major V H Simson + Squadron taken over the left half of 2nd Cav Brigade, undertakes reco of 3rd Cav Division who come in as part of the sector. Immediate 7 3rd Cav Division area are Northern boundary line is Sheet 57C.SE – X.18.c.9.8 – X.16.c.0.8. – X.19.c.8.0 – W.29.d.9.5. Search Southern boundary Sheet – 62c N.E. F.6.c.5.2. – F.4.c.8.0. – F.8.c.5.0. E.23 central Capt Corser born with 2nd Div HQ. + running line for his division	
	25th-28th		At F.4.b.1.3. 20 RE 20 Cav employed a dugout made by demolishing 180th Tun. Coy. RE. X.21.c.8.3. " 40 RE. 20 " " " F.16.7.1 " 20 RE. 20 " " " Dugout started by Peterson assisted by 180 Tun Coy. F.4.b.18. well completed in 25' Dugout of Cav. 13ch HQ.	

2353 Wt. W2544/1454 700,000 5/15 D. D. & L. A.D.S.S./Forms/C. 2118.

WAR DIARY or INTELLIGENCE SUMMARY

Army Form C. 2118.

3rd FIELD SQUADRON R.E. May 1917

Place	Date	Hour	Summary of Events and Information	Remarks and references to Appendices
	23-28		Outposts in ND, Section posts G & J echelons as follows Post G, F 5 c.	Sheet 61 NE
			Post H, X 28 c d	F4b Sheet 62 NE
			Post J, X 28 c d	Sheet 57 SE
			Work consists of Drainage, wiring, lateral communication + construction of MG emplacements.	
			Outposts in ND2 Section posts K L M Schedule as follows Post K X 22 c.	Sheet 57 SE
			" L X 22 c	57 SE
			" M X 21 c	57 SE
			Work consists of Drainage, wiring, lateral communication + construction of MG emplacements.	
	27-28		15 RE. 25 Cav divisional HQ at E 16 c NW VILLERS-FAUCON.	
	24-28		4 " 20 Cav camouflage road from ST EMILIE to EPEHY.	
			1 RE. 200 Cav making communication trench from X 21 d 0.8 - X 21 b Sheet 57 SE.	
			1 RE 100 " making communication trench from F 4 c 18 - F 4 b Sheet 62 NW.	
			from F 4 b 32 - F 5 c	"

W.A.H. Evans
O.C. 3rd Field Squadron R.E.

3rd Field Squadron

Army Form C. 2118.

WAR DIARY
or
INTELLIGENCE SUMMARY.
(Erase heading not required.)

June 1917.

Place	Date	Hour	Summary of Events and Information	Remarks and references to Appendices
	1-2		Sheet 57° SE	
		No 4 X 17 c.	12 RE + 160 Cavalry wiring front 2 section outpost situated at No1 par X17c: No2 X23a: No3 X24a. Wire consists of continuous apron fence.	
			12 RE + 110 Cav digging communication trench from BIRDCAGE (X 25 @ Sheet 57°SE) to Quarry (X29c Sheet 57°SE) previous scheme.	
			2 OS + 60 Cav digging support trench from front M situated (X21b Sheet 57°SE) to post L situated (X21d Sheet 57°SE)	
	2/3.		2 RE + 6 OR erecting Shrine hutch (hut) at EPEHY.	
			12 RE + 160 Cav continued wiring D2 Sector outposts numerals above.	
			12 RE + 70 Cav " " CT from Birdcage to Quarry as above.	
	2.		20 Cav 41 RE trench in CT (communication trench) to H par situated F4 b Sheet 62°NE	
	3/4.		4 RE + 70 Cav digging communication trench from Quarry to BIRDCAGE as above.	
		9 " 60	Wiring above communication trench.	
		12 " 100	Wiring from G par situated at F5c Sheet 62°NE to Quarry	
			Situated F 6 a Sheet 62°NE.	
			20 RE 432 Cav digging communication trench from 4 par situated (X21d Sheet 57°SE)	
			to outpost H a. Situated at X22d 7.7.	

W L W [signature]

2353 Wt. W25+4/1454 700,000 5/15 D. D. & L. A.D.S.S./Forms/C. 2118.

Army Form C. 2118.

WAR DIARY
or
INTELLIGENCE SUMMARY.
(Erase heading not required.)

JUNE 1917

Instructions regarding War Diaries and Intelligence Summaries are contained in F.S. Regs., Part II. and the Staff Manual respectively. Title pages will be prepared in manuscript.

Place	Date	Hour	Summary of Events and Information	Remarks and references to Appendices
	4/5		4 RE + 130 Cavalry digging communication trench from Quarry to BIRDCAGE as above	
		9 RE + 60 "	wiring same communication trench	
		12 " + 240 "	wiring from 6 post to Quarry as above	
		20 + 180 "	digging communication trench from L post to outpost line as above	
	5/6	10 RE + 120 Cav.	wiring Com. 6 post to Quarry as above, to trench with dam that they may be relief generally	
	6/7	4 RE + 160 Cav.	digging communication trench from Quarry to BIRDCAGE as above	
		16 " + 80 "	wiring same communication	
		16 " + 140 "	wiring from 6 post to Quarry as above	
		40 + 660 "	Digging communication trench from L post line outpost line as above	
	7/8	12 RE + 110 Cav.	Digging new communication from Quarry to Birdcage	
		20 " + 150 "	Digging communication trench from L post to outpost line	
		20 " + 270 "	Digging communication trench from F4 d 99 to Quarry	
	9/10	2 " + 40	Drawing Communication trench to 6 post + Camp trench to Subsection	
		20 " + 250	Digging communication trench Com L post + Camp trench to Subsection	

HQ at Pigeon Ravine Situated in X27 a Sheet 57 c SE
Wt. Ellis Capt RE

Army Form C. 2118.

WAR DIARY
or
INTELLIGENCE SUMMARY.
(Erase heading not required.)

June 1917

Place	Date	Hour	Summary of Events and Information	Remarks and references to Appendices
	3-7		4RE & 30 Cav Enemy camouflage seen at S entrance to ZPPEH on ST EMILIE to EPEHY road.	
	3-10		1RE officers from 10th Hussars & 30 Cav went on recce between ST EMILIE & VILLERS-FAUCON. Enemy Mg post entanglement between M post Trenches X21.b Sheet 57 S.E. & old infantry in X15.d Sheet 57 S.E. Drawn communication trench when runs from M post trench to Willows X21.a.	
	10-17		2 Sgts communication trench from L to Sunken road in X22.d. Work from 1K post situated X21.d Sheet 57 S.E. to Sunken road up to X22.d 8.5 + 6 No 1 M post situated in X23.c. Sheet 57 S.E. Drawn communication trench South of CATELET COPSE. Wiring 3rd & alg top of trench from CATELET COPSE trench as S.V.S. wood in X28.d. Wire any entanglement in front of No 6 post in X17.c.	

M.C.M. Capt. R.E.

Army Form C. 2118.

WAR DIARY
or
INTELLIGENCE SUMMARY.
(Erase heading not required.)

JUNE 1917.

Place	Date	Hour	Summary of Events and Information	Remarks and references to Appendices
	17-24		Improved communication trench Cmk park trunk unit X 22 ct d. Completed new front line parts No 1 outposts, also up in front. Started saphine emplacement between No 1 + 2 outposts. Finished diving communication trench S of CATARET COPSE. Drainage communication trench b-q Post + long trench trench. Diggin emplacement trench from BIRDCAGE to Quarry h X 29 d 43. Wiring same. 9 Trench mortar emplacements dug + one had been erected. BIRDCAGE.	
	25		1 O.Sappers + 2 NCOs accompanied cavalry raid party into BIRDCAGE. Torpedoes to destroy the enemy wire. Party superintended laying of same.	
	24-29		Continues work numeralation. Reyrouts Squadron horselines at BUIRE.	

M L McCaffre

Army Form C. 2118.

3rd FIELD SQUADRON, R.E.

WAR DIARY
or
INTELLIGENCE SUMMARY.
(Erase heading not required.)

O.O. 3rd Field Squadron R.E. JULY 1917.

Vol 37

Place	Date	Hour	Summary of Events and Information	Remarks and references to Appendices
	1st		Squadron at BUIRE.	
	3rd		Squadron leaves BUIRE for SUZANNE. LT WHEATLEY and 32 ORs join 2nd Field Sqdn RE.	
	4th		Squadron leaves SUZANNE for VILLE-SOUS-CORBIE.	
	5th		Squadron leaves VILLE-SOUS-CORBIE for FRESCHVILLERS.	
	6th		Squadron leaves FRESCHVILLERS for REBREUVIETTE.	
	7th		Squadron leaves REBREUVIETTE for BOURS.	
	10th		LT WHEATLEY & 32 ORs rejoin unit from 2nd Field Squadron RE.	
	16th		Squadron leaves BOURS for BUSNES.	
	22nd		Squadron leaves BUSNES for CAISTRE	
	27th		Squadron leaves CAISTRE for M.2.b.28. Sheet 28 1/40,000.	
	28th-31st		Squadron preparing water-supply for proposed Brigade camps.	

A.A. + Q.M.G.
3rd Cav Div.

Herewith War Diary for month of August.

[signature]
Major, R.E.
O.C. 3rd Field Squadron R.E.

3rd
FIELD SQUADRON
R.E.
SEPT. -8 1917

Army Form C. 2118.

3rd Field Squadron

WAR DIARY
or
INTELLIGENCE SUMMARY.
(Erase heading not required.)

August 1917

J51 3 2

Instructions regarding War Diaries and Intelligence Summaries are contained in F. S. Regs., Part II. and the Staff Manual respectively. Title pages will be prepared in manuscript.

Place	Date	Hour	Summary of Events and Information	Remarks and references to Appendices
	4/8/17		Preparing Camp for Cavalry Corps Headquarters at DICKEBUSCH Erecting horse lines & standings for horses in reserve Bde area	
	5/8/17		Preparing camp for Cavalry Corps Headquarters at DICKEBUSCH Erecting horse lines & standings in reserve Bde area	
	6/8/17		Preparing Camp for Cavalry Corps Headquarters at DICKEBUSCH	
	7/8/17		Preparing camp for Cavalry Corps Headquarters at DICKEBUSCH Repairing roadway leading to 1st Cav Bde Area (proposed) Repairs & replacing material	
	8/8/17		Commenced hut – Reinforcement camp at BAILLEUL	
	9/8/17		Continued hut – Reinforcement camp at BAILLEUL	
	10-31		Continued repairing horse standings Extensive rebuilding of 1st, 2nd & 3rd Cav Bdes & preparations for new huts at	
	28.11.		Strenging of photographers Erecting standings for horse lines at La CLYTTE under direction of II Corps and made Railway near Reninghelst + Siding Camp	

W.C.W. Capt RE

WAR DIARY
~~INTELLIGENCE~~ **SUMMARY.**
(Erase heading not required.)

3rd FIELD SQUADRON R.E.

Army Form C. 2118.

No. S.444

September 1917

Vol 33

Place	Date	Hour	Summary of Events and Information	Remarks and references to Appendices
Field	1/9/17		Cav: Corps Horse Show.	
	2/9/17 to 15/9/17		Building new Horse Clipping Depôt at WESTOUTRE and ZEVECOTEN to clip 20 horses at a time, power to be supplied by petrol engine.	
	16/9/17 to 28/9/17		Building new Horse Clipping Depôt at METEREN and Installing for 120 horses. Laying pipe line to ARAGON CAMP.	
	29/9/17 30/9/17		Preparing to install filter beds to purify water taken from DICKEBUSCH LAKE.	

J.P. Buchanan
Maj. R.E.

O.C. 3rd Field Squadron R.E.
30/9/17

Army Form C. 2118.

WAR DIARY
or
INTELLIGENCE SUMMARY.
(Erase heading not required.)

3rd FIELD SQUADRON, R.E.

No. a 3470
Mar 8/17

WA 34

October 17

Instructions regarding War Diaries and Intelligence Summaries are contained in F. S. Regs., Part II. and the Staff Manual respectively. Title pages will be prepared in manuscript.

Place	Date	Hour	Summary of Events and Information	Remarks and references to Appendices
I	1/10/17 to 5/10/17		Building filter beds at DICKEBUSCH LAKE to filter water before pumping it to forward area.	
	6/10/17 to 12/10/17		Building felt bags at DICKEBUSCH LAKE and erecting new camp for Corps Engr HQ at POPERINGHE.	
	13/10/17 to 16/10/17		Building filter beds at DICKEBUSCH LAKE and laying screens round intake pipes.	
	17/10/17 to 18/10/17		Dismantling Corps RE Camp at POPERINGHE. Erecting screens and building filter beds at DICKEBUSCH LAKE.	
	19/10/17		Marched WESTOUTRE to St FLORIS	
	20/10/17		Marched St FLORIS to MAREST	
	21/10/17		" MAREST to GRAND BOURET	
	22/10/17		" GRAND BOURET to CANAPLES	
	23/10/17		" CANAPLES to CORBIE	
	24/10/17		" CORBIE to DOINGT.	
	25/10/17 to 31/10/17		Hutting by 3rd Cav. B.D. at FLAMICOURT, BUIRE COURCELLES, DOINGT and LE MESNIL	

OC 3rd Field Squadron R.E.

Army Form C. 2118.

WAR DIARY
or
INTELLIGENCE SUMMARY.
(Erase heading not required.)

3 Fd Sqd R.E.

November 1917 Vol 35

Instructions regarding War Diaries and Intelligence Summaries are contained in F.S. Regs., Part II. and the Staff Manual respectively. Title pages will be prepared in manuscript.

Place	Date	Hour	Summary of Events and Information	Remarks and references to Appendices
	14/11		Erection of camps & stables for 3rd Cav Division at Domqt Courcelles, Flamicourt, Buire & Le Mesnil.	
	18			
	13/11		Moved from Domqt to Etinehem.	
	14		Lt Wheatley and 8 other ranks engaged on water supply at farms.	
	19/11 to 20/11		Squadron expecting to move at short notice in connection with attack on Cambrai.	
	22/11		Lt Maconochie & 15 other ranks to Gouzeaucourt	
	18		Lt Maconochie & 7 other ranks loaded bridging material on Tanks and proceeded to forward assembly point	
	19		Lt Maconochie proceeded to Marrieres – Bridge over Canal de l'Escaut completed by 11.30 A.M. & party returned to Gouzeaucourt.	
	20			
	21		Squadron moved from Etinehem to Domqt Bonneville	
	23		Squadron moved from Bonneville to Corbie	
	27		" " " Corbie to Domqt	
	28			
	29/11		Work at camps and stables for 3rd Cav Div. at Domqt, Courcelles, Buire, Le Mesnil & Flamicourt.	
	30/11			

D. Maconochie
Lt. R.E. for
O.C. 3rd Field Squadron R.E.

3rd FIELD SQUADRON, R.E.
No 9/14/17
S361

WAR DIARY
or
INTELLIGENCE SUMMARY

Army Form C. 2118.

3rd FIELD SQUADRON. R.E.

No. S.3877

December 1917

Place	Date	Hour	Summary of Events and Information	Remarks and references to Appendices
	1-6		Work at Camps and alteration for Cav. Sqn at DOIGNT - COURCELLES - BUIRE - LE MESNIL - FLAMICOURT.	
	2		20 ORs proceeded to VILLERS FAUCON to build Camp.	
		6-31	Work on defences between GRAND TRIEL WOODS & RIVER OMIGNON.	
	28/11/17		No 19550 Sapper (act. Pair L/Cpl) HOOK.H. } Awarded Military Medal	
			No 25285 " (") WITHEY.E.W. } 4 Cav Corps Commanders authority No AMS/500/141 28/11/17
	3/12/17		2/Lieut Macrochie H.D. Awarded the Military Cross Authority Cav Corps Commander AMS 500/141 3/12/17	

W.L.M Capt R.E.
O.C. 3rd Field Squadron R.E.

Army Form C. 2118.

WAR DIARY
or
INTELLIGENCE SUMMARY

3 - 3rd Sqdn
JANUARY 1918

Vol 37

Place	Date	Hour	Summary of Events and Information	Remarks and references to Appendices
O'MIGNON	1-15		Working on the # defences between GRAND PRIEL WOODS and the river O'MIGNON.	
	15		Squadron moved from MONS en CHAUSSÉE to FLAMICOURT.	
	17-31		1 Officer & 10 ORs moved to BUIRE for work in huts & baths in that area.	
	18-31		15 ORs moved to LE MESNIL for work in huts & baths in that area.	
	15		Remainder of Squadron working on huts &c at FLAMICOURT and Major E. Buchanan near H.R.E. School Instruction at BLENDECQUES.	

M R Chilgren

WAR DIARY 3rd Field Squadron R.E. Army Form C. 2118.
February 1918.

VII 38

Place	Date	Hour	Summary of Events and Information	Remarks and references to Appendices
FLAMICORT	1st to 28th		Squadron employed on erection of new huts, stables, cookhouse, baths - ablution sheds etc - repair of old huts in area - ① FLAMICORT - BUIRE - LE MESNIL - area ② MONCHY-LAGACHE - MONTECOURT - CAULINCOURT - TREFCON. Railway bridges (10) between DOINGT - PERONNE - LA CHAPELETTE - 9 road bridges (6) at BRIE prepared for demolition - Squadron attached to 1st Cavalry Division during whole month - 1 Officer & 9 O.R.s attached to 5th Field Squadron at TREFCON to work in area ② above -	
	3rd		No 14980 Sgt a/SSM CROCKETT.B. awarded Belgian CROIX de GUERRE. 3rd Cav Div. a/6953/5. d. 3.2.18) (authority)	
	19th		Major C.F. CARSON MC R.E. arrived from 17th Corps troops to command unit. Major E.J.B. BUCHANAN R.E. left to command 5th Field Squadron,	
	24th		Lt. R.F. JONES R.E. to Cavalry Corps Bridging Park & to command)	

WAR DIARY or INTELLIGENCE SUMMARY.

3rd Field Squadron RE Army Form C. 2118.

FEBRUARY 1918

Place	Date	Hour	Summary of Events and Information	Remarks and references to Appendices
FLAMICOURT	26th		2 Lt. H.A. BAZLEY RE. joined squadron from Base. 4 Officers & 33 O.Rs. on leave to U.K. during month.	

G.C. Gwinn-Sth
Capt RE
3 Field Squad

Army Form C.2118.
3rd FIELD SQUADRON. R.E

WAR DIARY
or
INTELLIGENCE SUMMARY.
(Erase heading not required.)

3rd Field Squadron R.E.

Vol 39

March 1918

Instructions regarding War Diaries and Intelligence Summaries are contained in F.S. Regs., Part II and the Staff Manual respectively. Title pages will be prepared in manuscript.

Place	Date	Hour	Summary of Events and Information	Remarks and references to Appendices
Flamicourt	March 1918 1-3-18		Squadron working on Hutting, improving shelters and preparation of bridges for demolition.	
	7.3.18		Bridges at PERONNE, FLAMICOURT (including) & CHAPELLETTE (including) prepared for demolition and handed over to 281 A.T. Coy; Bridge at BRIE (12) and at ETERPIGNY (2) prepared and handed over to 239 A.T.Coy R.E. Tank Hutment camp (30 huts) at DONNGT complete	
	8/12		Squadron moved to TERTRY - coming again into 3rd Cav Divn	
	13		Hutting & Stables	
	14-20		TERTRY to FOURQUES	
	21st		Work on Green line - working parties of 300 each from Canadian & 7th Bdes & 5th Bde	
	22nd		Moved under 3rd Cav Divn Orders to BEAUMONT	
	23rd		" " " " to BRETIGNY	
	25th		" " " " to CARLEPONT	
	26 "		" " " " to CAISNES	
			" " " " Bois de CARLEPONT	
			assisted French in demolition of two bridges at PONTOISE Railway Bridge and one Suspension Bridge of 160 ft span. 1st attempt French made fails in missing combustibles in afternoon completely successful	

Army Form C. 2118.

WAR DIARY
or
INTELLIGENCE SUMMARY.
(Erase heading not required.)

Place	Date	Hour	Summary of Events and Information	Remarks and references to Appendices
	March 1918 2.7		Marchendi 3rd Cav Div Orders to COMPEIGNE " " " " to GLORIETTE " " " " to SAINS-EN-AMIENOIS at SAINS Transfers of officers during month Capt Cobb to 203 Field Company 1-3-18 Lt Bristed to Forways Coy 10-3-18 Lt Boyce joined from 1st Field Squadron 6-3-18 Capt Grimsdale joined from 5th Field Squadron 7-3-18	

3rd Cav.Div.

WAR DIARY

3rd FIELD SQUADRON, R.E.

APRIL

1918

INTELLIGENCE SUMMARY.

(Erase heading not required.)

Vol 40

April, 1918

Summaries are contained in F.S. Regs., Part II. and the Staff Manual respectively. Title pages will be prepared in manuscript.

Place	Date	Hour	Summary of Events and Information	Remarks and references to Appendices
	27th		Digging and wiring the GENTELLES - CACHY Switch about 2500 long. Rifle pits were dug as a front line on a double apron fence of wire uncut. Support line similarly dug and 3 posts as a Reserve line. Support line and wiring at Support line and went on as usual on evening of two support as a continuing the rest of Reserve and two of Complete defence directly at S.E. of CACHY, who was not complete as the squadron was withdrawn to the night at the 8 p.m. to rejoin the Brigade at RIVERY. Squadron marched from RIVERY to NEUVILLE.	
"	"		NEUVILLE to BOYAVAL	
"	12		BOYAVAL to SAINS-LEZ-PERNES	
"	14		Squadron at SAINS-LEZ-PERNES, halt at 3.35 hour march to new Squadron was carried out by the following Lorries on 2nd Dragoons and machinery	
	14.30			
			Transfers of Officers during month.	
			Lieut. L.E. Lynedale, R.Q. to 156 u gulu Bryst R.Q. 7th Lut by M. Fairbrough, R.Q.(O.f.) from 8 gen 24 to 2nd Life Gds. 9th	
			Awards	
			38411 Cpl Simonds A. awarded military medal on 6.2.1918 London Gazette No.11 of 1918 A.C. 2nd Life Gds	

Army Form C. 2118.

WAR DIARY
or
INTELLIGENCE SUMMARY. 3rd W. Field Squadron R.E.
3rd Cav. Div.
(Erase heading not required.)

Vol 4

May 1918

Place	Date	Hour	Summary of Events and Information	Remarks and references to Appendices
SAINS les PERNES	May 1-3		Division still at 3½ hours notice to move. Training was continued in Elementary Musketry, Fire Control, Foot Drill.	
	4		Warning order received night of 3rd that Div would move next day	
	5		Moved to OEUF YVREMCHEUX	
	6		" BEHENCOURT — an attack was expected and the Field Squadron with 360 cavalry men were provided to work nightly. By 6 p.m. that evening the instructions of Corps thro' 47th Div but at 6 pm that was cancelled & we were switched to fresh work in front of HENENCOURT. Same night dug over 1200× of trench in the shape of rifle pits over the COPSE COURT line.	C.R.E.
	7		Reconnoitred made C.E. Corps & took charge of Defences E & N of HENENCOURT	
	8		Continued to work under full pressure on these defences up to & including 16th	
			Working parties 1st two days 360 men daily length that 450 men daily. Tasks given digging 3½ yds of Trench 3' at top 2' at bottom and 3'6 deep using 20 yards double apron fence per man.	
			A new line of wire always started by digging rifle pits 7 yds long and at 14 yards interval; when available wire was put up concurrently	

Army Form C. 2118.

WAR DIARY
or
INTELLIGENCE SUMMARY.
(Erase heading not required.)

Instructions regarding War Diaries and Intelligence Summaries are contained in F. S. Regs., Part II. and the Staff Manual respectively. Title pages will be prepared in manuscript.

Place	Date	Hour	Summary of Events and Information	Remarks and references to Appendices
			Wire was kept as far as possible 60' and over from trenches. [sketch of trench profile with measurements: ←7'→, 1st Task, ←7'→, picked up later, +1', ←3'→, ←2'→, -38'-, -6'-] Map attached shews detail of work completed and in hand when Division was drawn on 1)TH. Work was continued by 1 troop of F. Squadron of 1 Cavalry Bde supplying 150 men daily left at Behencourt for that purpose.	

WAR DIARY or INTELLIGENCE SUMMARY

Army Form C. 2118.

Place	Date	Hour	Summary of Events and Information	Remarks and references to Appendices
			COPSE, COURT, JAKES, POSSUM became the main line of defence	
			CAVALRY TRACK, a switch across the valley to the WARLOY sector and TERRACE TRENCH to cover the SENLIS valley & its TERRACE Switches as shown hereon dotted) north of & blue south of HENENCOURT back to Warloy system as part of HENENCOURT DEFENCES	
	17th		Division less Can Car Bde (with Squadron less 3rd Field Troop (attached to Can. Car. Bde) marched to training area about ST OEUN & BELLOY 3rd Fd Squadron billets & bivouaced at BETTENCOURT (St. OEUN)	
	18-31		Training Musketry; Map Reading and Troop Drill chiefly	
	24th		2nd Troop (attached to 7 Cav Bde) relieved 3rd Troop on Terrace Work	
	3rd		1st " " " " " 2nd " " " " "	
			Transfer of Officers during month.	
			Lt. C.R. Boyce R.G. to 152 M.G. from Coy R.G. 14-5-18	
			Capt. G.H. Fairburgh to L.233rd Bat. or Bat. R.G. 21-5-18	
			Capt. R.D. Alexander from 1st Bde Canadian 14-5-18	
			Lt. F.G. Bennett joined unit on 23-5-18	
			Awards.	
			Capt. G.H. Fairburgh awarded Military Cross L.G. 19 Corps Order no. 13 of 1-7-18	

J. Carson
Major R.E.
O.C. 3rd Fd Canadian
Field Squadron

STATEMENT OF WORK DONE BY
II FIELD TROOP & 150 CAM. CAV. BDE
FOR WEEK 17.5.18 to 23.5.18.

Location of Work.	Work Done.
V16d (2-3) to V21b (9-9) V22b (7-9)	1,250 yds Trench dug connecting CAV TRENCH, TERRACE to JAKES SUPPORT. JAKES SUPPORT connected up.
From Road V15d (4-8) V16c (1-3) to V15d (6-0)	600 yds double apron fence & connecting wire of CAV TRENCH to TERRACE TRENCH.
V16c (2-4) to V22b (7-9)	Second belt of wire completed in front of TERRACE TRENCH 1,000 yds.
V29b (3-7) V24c (9-4)	Double apron fence in front of JAKES OBSERVATION carried on 1,000 yds to WATTLE ST & THE MAZE
V23b (3)	4 Gun M.G. post HAM REDOUBT completely camouflaged
V21b (8-5)	4 " " " " completed
V16c (7-4)	2 " " " " camouflaged.
V22b (35-55) to 200yds to West V22c (5-6) to L4a (2-8).	1,200 yds Trench dug & connected up making COURT SUPPORT complete.

J. D. Maconochie
Lt. R.E.

Trenches Continuous. ———
   "   When Rifle Pits are dug — - — -
   "   Projected - Work not started ....
Wire double apron ××××××××
Trenches by 5th Corp. ———
Machine Guns oooo ∞ 4 Guns & 2 Guns.

FIELD SQUADRON
Army Form C. 2118.

WAR DIARY
or
INTELLIGENCE SUMMARY.
(Erase heading not required.)

June 1918   3rd Field Squadron R.E.

Instructions regarding War Diaries and Intelligence Summaries are contained in F.S. Regs., Part II. and the Staff Manual respectively. Title pages will be prepared in manuscript.

Place	Date	Hour	Summary of Events and Information	Remarks and references to Appendices
	1-6-18 to 30-6-18		The work in the forward area was continued by one Troop with one Brigade of Cavalry. The 2nd Troop with Lt Wheatley in Command relieved the 1st Troop on the 14th — (2nd Troop attached to 7th Bde.) Lt Wheatley was relieved by Lt Ray on 21st. An relief of 2nd Bde Can Bde. on the 21st the 2nd Troop came under Canadian Bde. As the defences in front of and around Hénencourt advanced the work was extended southwards. Training at BETTENCOURT was carried on continuously in Map Reading, Field Geometry etc Pontooning, Musketry and Equitation.	

R.H.Q. casualties
18.2.19 3pm Nicks/Monkhouse F. Nr 94445 wounded by shell 2pounder 3 to 78
10.990.   (Remained on duty.)
Cripps R.   Sappers (Officers)   — do — 94618

Capt. H.H. Morgenzie C.R.E. N.C.F. F.D.I. 9 mb. 11.98 = Lt S.S. Bennett R.E. to Gr Ops
Lt R.E. Arbuckle to Co. Capt. Cran 11.6.18 - 3/4 FSy Ky R.E. to 330 Fd Sq 18/18
Capt G Best B.R. to 3rd FD Sq. 24.6.18.

A.Caron
O.C. 3rd Field Squadron R.E.

Army Form C. 2118.

WAR DIARY
or
INTELLIGENCE SUMMARY.
(Erase heading not required.)

Vol 43 3rd Field Squadron July 1918.

Instructions regarding War Diaries and Intelligence Summaries are contained in F.S. Regs., Part II. and the Staff Manual respectively. Title pages will be prepared in manuscript.

Place	Date	Hour	Summary of Events and Information	Remarks and references to Appendices
	1/7/18 to 3/7/18		Training of N.C.O's and men in Map Reading and musketry carried out at BETTENCOURT ST OUEN.	
	1/7/18 to 6/7/18		One Troop attached to Canadian Cav. Bde. employed on improving defences in LAVIEVILLE. Detach. from 9.10 to D.16. Sheet 62.D Two troops rejoined unit at DREUIL on the 5th inst.	
	3rd		Sheet 62 E & F. 32. C.1.3. Squadron less No. 2 Troop moved to DREUIL.	
	4/7/18 to 29/7/18		Unit employed by R.E. 9 Cdn. B. & 8th Div. — Work was carried out on the F.N. (Forward North) defs. of the G.H.Q. line — line from B. & central to L.33.b. Sheet 62 E by three parties. The approximate daily strength of each party being 10.20 sappers and 80 OR. (Chinese) Work throughout period was greatly hampered owing to P.U.O. Casualties.	
			Left Sub Sector Front line from track at R.12. central to railway at R.3. wired with 2 belts of double apron three and tactical wire. Trench near quarry in R.2.b. wired with two belts. Hell's Trench in gravel pit L.33. wired with two belts of double apron. Switch trench in R.2.a. & of road wired with single apron fence. "N." wired with one belt of double apron fence. "M." wired with one belt of double apron fence.	
			R.I.B.S. All gaps for Artillery and Infantry in front line of wire were provided with knife rests.	
			Right half of F.N. Sector. Two double apron fences complete with tactical wire every 50'+ from B.8.D to R.12. central gaps every 150'+ were provided with knife rests for Infantry, gaps every 150'+ were provided with knife rests.	

WAR DIARY
or
INTELLIGENCE SUMMARY.

Army Form C. 2118.

Sheet IV

Place	Date	Hour	Summary of Events and Information	Remarks and references to Appendices
	27/8 to 29/8		The Brown line from R.9.d. to B.11.b. wired with 3 different types of experimental wire Support line from R.9.a. to R.29.a. wired with gaps every 150+. Brown line running from Q.5.d. to K.29.d. wired with double apron fence. From Q.6. central to K.35.b. wired with plain fence. Sketch of Bn Sub sector attached.	
	30/7/18		Squadron moved back to BETTENCOURT ST OUEN. Movements of Officers during month. 2/Lieut. H. A. Bagley R.E. to hospital 22.7.18. Capt. A.K. Grant. Rams Bdgs.10, 309 Bn. — 9th 12/7/18 Capt. G.J. Neil Rams from 7 Cav. B.D. 12/7/18 Capt. H.A. Bagley R.E. from hospital 25/7/18 2/Lt. Capt. A.K. Grant Rams from hosp. 2/gn. 31/7/18. Capt. G.J. Neil. R.A.M.C. to 7th Bn. J.A. 31/7/18	

W.O.C. 3rd Field Squadron R.E.

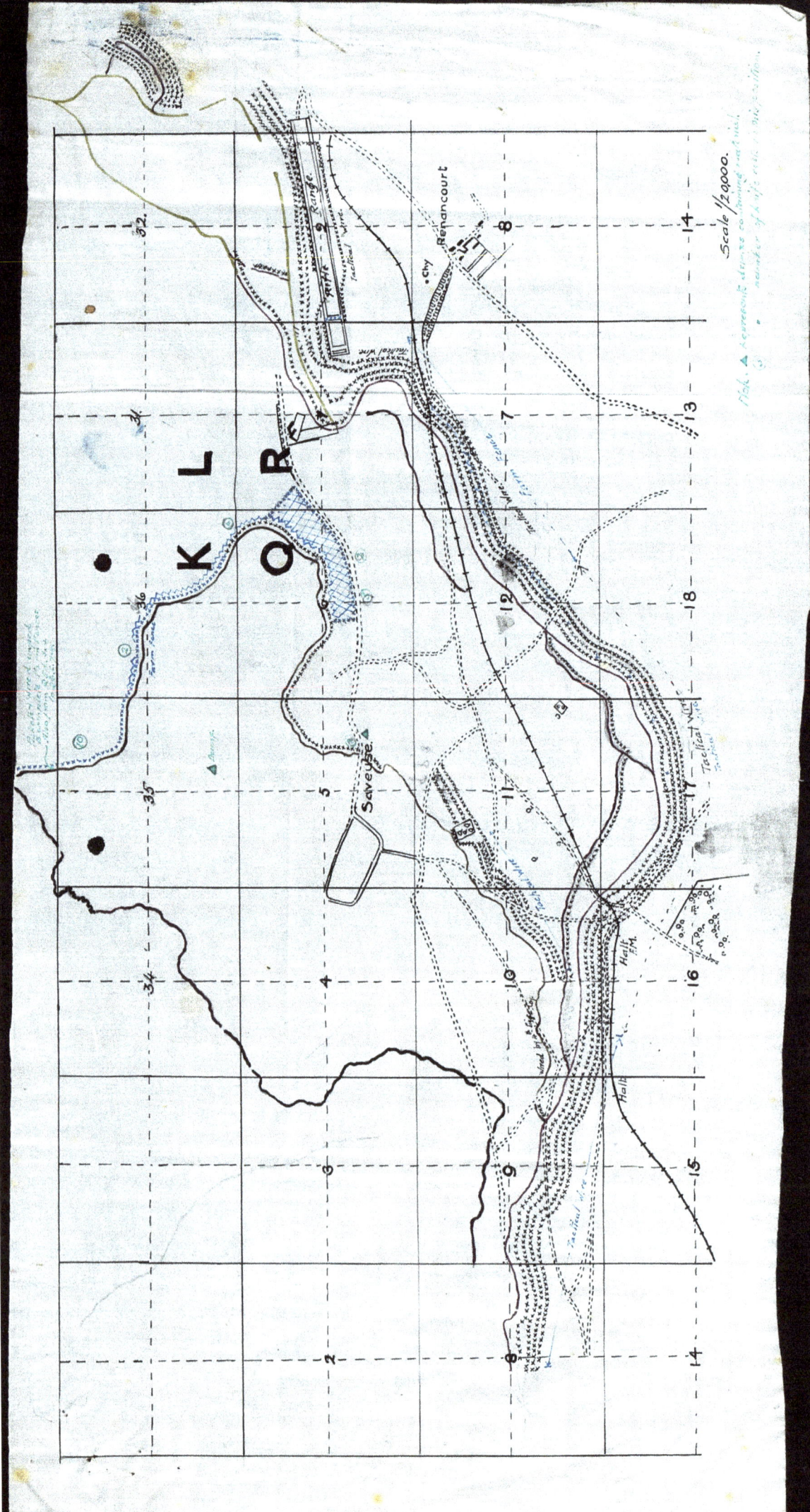

Army Form C. 2118.

WAR DIARY 3rd Field Sq. R.E.

INTELLIGENCE SUMMARY.
(Erase heading not required.)

1st August 1918

Place	Date	Hour	Summary of Events and Information	Remarks and references to Appendices
BETTENCOURT	August 1918 1–6		Squadron was to go to AUXI-le-CHATEAU for Bridging but this move was disallowed. The reason was soon to be made known. On 4th O.C. reconnoitred with G.O.C. Divn. a cavalry track route thro' our own system of trenches East of AMIENS. Track was to start from near BOIS de TRONVILLE on the ST NICHOLAS – BLANGY-TRONVILLE Road. It had to go due east passing CACHY on the NORTH side and after crossing our front line, to be taken forward to NORTH edge of MORGEMONT WOOD – Track 7500 x behind our front line and 3500 x in front had to be 20 x wide throughout. The operation – with the purpose of relieving the pressure on AMIENS – was prepared with such secrecy that no steps were allowed to be taken with regard to the track prior to the night preceding Zero – Work estimates 2 Coys American Engineers allotted on a working Party i.e. F Coy of 108th Battn. U.S. Engineers. Divn marched night of 6-7th to concentration Area W. of ARRAS. The Squadron to a position about 1 mile north of BOVES. During afternoon 7th reconnoitred line with Troop Leaders. Divided work 1st Troop 3500 x W. Party 75 men D Coy U.S.A. Engineers 2nd Troop 2000 x " " 65 " " 3rd Troop From CACHY to Front Line 1500 x Flashing Party F Coy 108 U.S.A Engineers 3rd Troop with F Coy Americans after completing to front line to await in Front Line trenches and go forward [crossed out] at Zero after the Canadian Troops who attacked. Track to be marked by triangular white flags (3') at tench [trench] guards at 50 x intervals	CJC

Army Form C. 2118.

WAR DIARY
or
INTELLIGENCE SUMMARY.

3rd Feb 18 Sq. R.E.

(Erase heading not required.)

Instructions regarding War Diaries and Intelligence Summaries are contained in F. S. Regs., Part II. and the Staff Manual respectively. Title pages will be prepared in manuscript.

Place	Date	Hour	Summary of Events and Information	Remarks and references to Appendices
East of AMIENS	August 1918 8th—	3 am approx	Work on track carried out satisfactorily being completed to Front Line at 3 am approx. 2nd and 3rd Troops rested to Assembly Area of Dun Wd BLANGY-TRONVILLE— BOVE'S Road, 3rd Troop with F Coy USA Engineer works forward to MORGEMONT WOOD Pluvine closely after attacking troops Zero hour was 4.20 am. 1st Squadron of Cavalry (L.S.H.) came through to MORGEMONT WOOD at about 8 am and whole Divn followed soon after. Horses of No 3 Troop were led forward by No 1 and No 2 Troops No 3 Troop joined A1 Echelon. Squadron came into Divn reserve and were not again actively employed. Casualties in making Track morning of 8th 3rd Troop 1 killed 2 wounded American Working Party 2 killed 10 wounded. Crossings of R Luce were reconnoitred at Aubercourt and Ignacourt Canadian Pole Crosses at Ignacourt soon after 7 am and were closely followed by 7th Cav Bde.	CJC
	9th—		night of 8th & 9th— Squadron in CAYEUX WOOD South end	
	10th—	night of 10th— at BEAUFORT— were to put up a waterpoint at BEAUFORT with equipment from Can Corps Bridging Park. A felt elevator with trestle lengths etc was sent up arriving on 11 a am. Point was not much use due was ordered to withdraw night of 11th & BOVES Area	
	11th—	10 pm	Squadron arrived at REMIENCOURT	

WAR DIARY 3rd Field Squadron R.E. Army Form C. 2118.
or
INTELLIGENCE SUMMARY

(Erase heading not required.)

Place	Date	Hour	Summary of Events and Information	Remarks and references to Appendices
	August 1918			
	12–15		at REMIENCOURT – B Echelon joined Squadron from SOUES on 12th–13th night. Chief work – cleaning billets and area	
	15th–18th		night 15th/16th Divn marched to old area ST OEUN HANGEST – Squadron to BETTENCOURT	
BETTENCOURT	16th			
ST OEUN	25th		From 21st at 3 hours notice to move 6th Cav Bde moved to FIEFFES Area, Can. Cav Bde to DOMART in position of readiness	
CAUMONT	25th		marched 9.30 pm for CAUMONT under Divn Orders	C/C
GALAMETZ	26th		" 7.15 pm to GALAMETZ – Divn to operate under 1st Army	
"	27th		Conference re operations Divn Hdqrs.	
"	29th		Advised to move to area W. of Arras – later cancelled	
"	30th		ditto ditto	
"	31st		Now at 6 hours notice to move. B Echelon rejoined today	

C N Carver Major R.E.

WAR DIARY or INTELLIGENCE SUMMARY

Army Form C. 2118.

Sept 1918

3rd Field Squadron R.E.

Place	Date	Hour	Summary of Events and Information	Remarks and references to Appendices
GALAMETZ	1–9		Training horses and Riding Drill	
CAUMONT	10–15		ditto. Scheme for Officers on demolitions especially of Railway and Evening Shows. Hurried Pioneer Instructor given to 6th & 7th Sdns at VIEL HESDIN	
Manœuvres	16–17		On 16th Moved to Le Parcq – on 17th Manœuvres of Can Corps. Sqdn right at WAVANS. 3rd Cav Divn was in support; special work of Squadron was to cut railway at CANDAS – Operations were ceased before 3rd Cav Divn came into action	
HARAVESNES	18–24		Moved to Haravesnes on 18th morning. Submitted programme for Pioneer course to Divn. Divn selected a complete course for each Brigade. I. Demolitions (1) without explosives (2) with explosives II. Bridging experiments. Ordered by divn on 21st to prepare to start classes on 23rd. It was arranged to do a Bridging Experiment at WAIL. Demolitions at FIEFVILLERS and TORTEL and a time table made out for Brigades – 1 Officer & 3 men per Squadron attended. Classes well started but on 24th Warning Order & move was received. Classes were suspended from same day to stow critically	

Army Form C. 2118.
R.E.

WAR DIARY
or
INTELLIGENCE SUMMARY. 3rd FUS Squad R.E.
(Erase heading not required.)

Instructions regarding War Diaries and Intelligence Summaries are contained in F.S. Regs., Part II. and the Staff Manual respectively. Title pages will be prepared in manuscript.

Place	Date	Hour	Summary of Events and Information	Remarks and references to Appendices
On Trek	25		Night March to VAOCHELLES Nr AUTHIE	
	26th		" " Position S.E. of ALBERT	
	27th		" " to CURLU	
	28		Resting at "	
	29th		Night MARCH to COULAINCOURT	

Awards.
Major C.F. Caron, R.E. - Bar to M.C. } Authority:
31371 Corpl. Coleman, E. - Bar to M.M. } Car Corps No. H.M.S. 500/347 (undated)

Officers - Arrivals & departures

Lieut E.A. Wheatley, R.E. to 122nd Field Coy. R.E. 7.9.18 Auth. A.G. No 55/6028 (D) of 1.9.18
Lieut K. Ray, R.E. to C.E. 2nd Army 23.9.18 Auth. Car Corps P4 FF00/436 of 20.9.18
2/Lt H. Mitchell, R.E. from R.E. Base Depot 8.9.18

C Mason Major R.E.
O.C. 3rd Fld Squad R.E.

October 1918

WAR DIARY of 3rd Field Squadron R.E.
INTELLIGENCE SUMMARY.
(Erase heading not required.)

Army Form C. 2118.

Vol 46

Place	Date	Hour	Summary of Events and Information	Remarks and references to Appendices
COULAINCOURT			On 25th Sept. Sqn. had moved to the POEUILLY-VERMAND area. Squadron was at COULAINCOURT. The day previous a conference had been held at Divn HQrs when an outline of the scheme of operation was discussed. Roughly the rôle of the Cavalry was to be as follows — Following an attack by the 1st 3rd and 4th Armies if after the 4th Army had secured the ground to north and east of BEAUREVOIR and MONTRENCUIN the enemy's resistance was broken and it was reported to be demoralized the cavalry Corps would pass through the 4th Corps's front and moving in the general direction of the main MARETZ — LE CATEAU Road seize the high ground to the north and east of LE CATEAU and be prepared to advance on and cut the railway communications at VALENCIENNES. The role of the Field Squadrons was the chief. The cutting of railway lines at BUSIGNY and LE CATEAU and WALENCIENNES and the destruction of Telegraph communications. At first only the N°1 & lines west of LE CATEAU were to be cut but later on the operations all Telegraph communications were to be destroyed. Other concentrated works were also discussed. We had before discussed the matter of destroying and of cutting or changing Railways and come to the conclusion, in the latter case of attack noise &	

Army Form C. 2118.

WAR DIARY or **INTELLIGENCE SUMMARY**

3rd Field Squadron R.E.

(Erase heading not required.)

October 1918

Place	Date	Hour	Summary of Events and Information	Remarks and references to Appendices
	Oct 1/18		with charges on the points and crossings and on the open line at the link pts (2 men 1 mayfale & appear and 2 cavalry) laid these charges at the rate of 20 per hour. On completing work 1st Cav Div moved up with the 3rd Cav Div following close. An S.O.S. Sept 1st F.S. Troop was attached to 6th Bde who were to do right flank. Hd. quarters moved to the 1st Cav Div.	
COULAIN-2nd COURT			Div. to assemble at daybreak east of VADENCOURT — conference at Div Hd Qrs at daybreak. During concentration orders of Cav Corps were altered making 3rd Cav Div leading Div with first part following — this was due to difficulty of the BELLICOURT CROSSING of CANAL & possibility which had been foreseen. It was necessary to see officers again and to send 2nd Troop to join up with 7th Cav Bde. However by the time this was done the operations so far as the Cav Corps were concerned were cancelled and the divn returned to same area.	
	3rd		Divn was again assembled but was moved east of Canal and was withdrawn at night. Squadron this time went to VERMAND where He was [illegible] until the morning of the 8th.	
	6th		Conference at Divn Hd Qrs meeting when it was decided to make at night to two cavalry Troops [illegible] just north of WIANCOURT-town line to BEAUREVOIR LINE one just north of road to WIANCOURT from HD Qrs South of JONCOURT to pass to South of WIANCOURT — (see attached sketch)	

WAR DIARY
INTELLIGENCE SUMMARY

Army Form C. 2118.

Place: October
Unit: "A" Field Squadron R.E.

Date	Hour	Summary of Events and Information	Remarks
Oct 7th		Cavalry Tracks were made and marked after dusk by white flags on long 2' poles.	
8th	3 p.m.	Div ordered to follow Canadian 18th in valley S.W. of JONCOURT. 3rd Troop attached 7th Cav Bde & 2nd Troop attached in valley S. of JONCOURT. 1st Troop was with drawn from 6th Bde and rejoined Squadron — Div moved up to BEAUREVOIR area in close touch behind 1st Cav Divn, but did not come into action. No further reconnaissances for water were made. 6th Div and 2nd Divn watered and GOUY but that area was all within 6½ miles of Divn watering areas. BELLICOURT - BELLENGLISE and Squadron had erected watering point and night on east bank of Canal south of BELLENGLISE.	
9th	3.00	Orders received to concentrate near main LECHATEAU Road east of BEAUREVOIR - Bde in position by 07.00 — O.C. to Divn to give orders for operation. Scheme of operation remained much the same but 3rd Cav Divn is now to be leading divn with 2nd Divn following. B "Field" Troop was thereafter drawn from Canadian 7th & 6th Cav Bdes & Sqn Hd rejoined with 7 Cav Bde.	
		Before emphasis was laid on the necessity of Troop leaders according to depth on Engineer Reconnaissance. This was the more urgent since th...	

Army Form C. 2118.

WAR DIARY

October 1918

INTELLIGENCE SUMMARY of 3rd Field Squadron R.E.

(Erase heading not required.)

Place	Date	Hour	Summary of Events and Information	Remarks and references to Appendices
	9.10.		The squads fell out/stood & finished Ph.G. the TT. attacked the Cav. Corps operated entirely for motor transport. All infantry objecting areas, much of the sand tracks to G.H.E., Cav. Corps and Gate Bole. Operations did not go deeply into enemy. Details were able to cut the railways & destroy telegraphs. During a period however the 2nd Troop much of a division fell to motor transport on main road of O.2.b.d. - a Telept about 20 prisoners were stopped and put on this work. Main road up Maurois was demolished at 09.15. The reserve Troop then I Tp. Hdqrs. was employed also on roads. No more advance of them to make. The way prepared for motor transport as ever. 3 craters were dealt with in Maurois. The biggest & roughest was at the crossing over Railway in P.27.B. S.W. of Maurois. Here the bridge had been completely destroyed leaving a 100 ft gap just this impossible. A diversion was made about 100 yds to south & round this the Station. The road here is in a rather high embankment. The demolition of the bridge was most complete, a lucky abutment. The road was shaken for a considerable distance leaving it broken on the eastern side. Sketch shown division.

Att(A) Ramp from platform and field across rails were made of timbers and such the rails | |

→ To Maurois.
Bonfield
← To Maurois

WAR DIARY of 3rd F.S. Squadron R.E.

INTELLIGENCE SUMMARY

Army Form C. 2118.

October 1918

Place	Date	Hour	Summary of Events and Information	Remarks and references to Appendices
	9th		A/H(B) left transport back on to road it was necessary to make a considerable filling which was necessitated with large forces from the demolished bridge. A party of about 30 prisoners were stopped on the way back and they materially assisted in pushing the job thro' quickly. It was about 17.45 when the Troop arrived on the road. In half an hour light ambulances were across and in an hour it was ready for motors. O.C. Car Car FC Ambulance also provided us with a working party until his ambulances crossed. Squadron afterwards withdrew for nights to P26B near Dun Hogas. 3rd Troops with 10th Hussars of 6th Cav Bde came under all the heavy M.G. and shell fire with result that 2 O.R's were wounded 2 horses killed 5 wounded and evacuated and several others wounded but which were kept at work.	
	10th		Dun attacked by 06.00 hrs in sally South of TROISVILLES, 1st RH Troop was sent to be told in relief of 3rd RH Troop. The Dun was across BELLE River but this was found impracticable so the 1st & 2nd Troops were little employed during the day. Early in the morning the road was reconnoitred up to the TROISVILLE - PROISVILLE road, this was reported to be fully held by civilians at the village	

WAR DIARY
INTELLIGENCE SUMMARY

of 3rd Fd Squadron R.E.

October 1918

Date	Hour	Summary of Events and Information
10		There was a large crater on TROISVILLE-REUMONT road at P.4.D.7.5 near the mill. The road here is in cutting and the way was completely blocked. A party of our Cyclist Goliath attacks to Bn Diaries filled this and the road was open same afternoon. The 3 N Troop of Squadron was kept employed on discharging mines – many breaches where mines were reported were reconnoitred. A road mine was de-charged at road junction south of Le TAYT P.4.B.2.5 and also charges were taken from the two level crossings at BERTRY. MONTIGNY and BERTRY was reconnoitred for water. Dam was ordered to be built about these places. One section Car Coys Watersupply, ordered up for erection at MONTIGNY. This section was built in assisting 2 units Divn Indian Watersupply in made by 0730 next morning at CLARY. Squadron bivouaced at MONTIGNY
11		Water Watersupply erected at ELINCOURT.
12		WATER POINT dismantled at CLARY and erected at MONTIGNY. This section proved very useful and the waterpoints were largely used by Infantry & RTA as well as Cavalry. Generally you should count on 2 hours to erect one of these installations. At Places water can actually be found in wells and even farm courtyards but only a limited number of horses can be dealt with before __

WAR DIARY for 3rd Cav. Brigade R.E.
INTELLIGENCE SUMMARY

Army Form C. 2118.

Place	Date	Hour	Summary of Events and Information	Remarks and references to Appendices
	13th		Wire installation is in order.	
	14th		Div. withdrawn – squadron marched to HONNECOURT on ST QUENTIN Canal	
	15th		" " " " " HONNOIS WOOD	
	to		Staffing of Sqdn and Division. General routine work for 3rd Division including instruction of Baths for 3rd & 7th Bdes. Upkeep of Plank Roads and Water Points in Divisional Area.	
	31st			
			Casualties In Action	
			134919 Sapper McCluskey, P. wounded 9.10.18	
			113909 " Ronson, W. -do-	
			101449 " Bodie, G.B. -do-	
			Remained at duty.	
			Movements of Officers	
			Capt. S.S. Lamb, C.A.M.C. – temporary attached – returned to Can. Cav. Fd. 5.10.18	
			" P.H. McCallum, R.A.M.C. joined unit as temporary 5.10.18	
			" J.C. Kinsey, R.A.M.C. rejoined unit from hospital 12.10.18.	
			" P.H. McCallum, R.A.M.C. to 6th Cav. F.A. 12.10.18.	
			Lieut. O.R. Lyster, R.E. joined unit as a reinforcement 22.10.18	
			2/Lt. F. Richardson, R.E. " " " 31.10.18	
			Lieut. O.R. Lyster, R.E. transferred to 90th Field Squadron, departed unit. 31.10.18	

R.W. Allinardi Capt. R.E.
O/C 3rd Field Squadron, R.E.
7.11.18.

Army Form C. 2118.

WAR DIARY
or
INTELLIGENCE SUMMARY

(Erase heading not required.)

Ref: No. 001 Sheets 11.12.5.6.

3rd FIELD SQUADRON R.E.

November Sheet I

Place	Date	Hour	Summary of Events and Information	Remarks and references to Appendices
	1st		HERMIES. Wood & horse shy work unaltered of general position. Work in Div area - Batta stabling etc. Drivain troops over water supply in Div Area - the remaining stations were still maintained by Water 3 lorries - and Div took over the repair etc. of AT RES Pipe line system and the maintenance in Borough etc.	
	4th		Warning order received to stand in readiness to move. Standing in readiness at 2½ hrs notice.	
	5th		Sqdn moved to INCHY-EN-ARTOIS via HAVRINCOURT & MOEUVRES & ELL accompanied	
	6th		Sqdn moved to WAGNONVILLE (VALENCIENNES Sheet 12) via DOUAI	
	7th		Sqdn moved to ATTICHES. Sht. 12. G.O.C. Div ordered search to be made for abandoned enemy delay action mines and dug outs in PHAEMPIN in which That Div. Lorry traffic could get through. Two mines were made in this village and Sht traffic was restored. N. This Sht. road - mines mines were found in ATTICHES and several parties were employed in removing and rendering same harmless. In this connection much information was obtained by the Interpreter (H Bay) from civilians of the location of these mines - as the civilians shut in many cases. Three mines were employed in their construction. Most of these mines were humming up the ½ special delay action fuse fuel and then inverted - others were connected up to the full electrically. Booby traps were also observed in some Billets near M. AVELIN & PERENNE (Sheet 12) These were destroyed with explosives - and some of type shown in Plate IV- "German Traps & Mines". Casualties from these traps occurred in this area	JR

WAR DIARY or INTELLIGENCE SUMMARY

Army Form C. 2118.

November 1918
FIELD SQUADRON R.E.

Sheet II

Ref 1/100,000 Sheets 11. 12. 5. 6.

Place	Date	Hour	Summary of Events and Information	Remarks and references to Appendices
	8th		Marching orders received for 1 Section to be attached to 9th Cav. Bde. for work north 11th/12th	
	9th		1 Section (from 2nd Troop) (LINCOLN wire) joined 9th Bde. en route for LA MADELEINE (Sh 12+15). CRE Cav Corps issued instructions re 1 employ in forthcoming operations. Plans R S T bridges over the strictly BLATON CANAL S of ATH (Sheet 5 - TOURNAI) Sqdn was latter notified of Cav Corps Bde. equipment 3rd Troop was sent to Div H.Q. for removal of mines in Bde. area. 1 Section of 1st Troop attached to Corp Bde. for mine removal in Bde. area. This Section also did much useful work and were very fully employed.	CR
	10th		Sqdn moved to vicinity of LA VERTE RUE. Unit consisted of 2 Troops and H.Q. plus 1 Section of each Troop detached for removal of mines in Bde. areas. 3rd Troop marched with Div H.Q. en route. Destruction was charged to RUMES (Sheet 5) and here 3rd Troop rejoined. 1 Section of 1st Troop was sent to 6th Bde H.Q. to meet with leading patrols for road reconnaissance. Later destinations was again changed to ANTOING (Sheet 5). 1 Section of Cav Corps Belg Park was attached to H.Q. Sqdn at RUMES and attached to H.Q. Sqdn.	
	11th		Conference at Div H.Q. Operation orders issued. Sqdn to move along general line :— VEZON – PONEVCHE – WILLAUPUIS – TOURPES – BLICQUY – ORMEIGNES – MAFFLE – GIBECQ SILLY (Ref Sheet 100,000 TOURNAI 5) 1st Troop attached to 6th Cav Bde. Sqdn less 2nd Troop and detached sections marched via FONTENOY to TOURPES where 3rd Troop joined Cav. Cav Bde. Information was received that Armistice was signed and that hostilities would occur at 11.00 hrs. This was confirmed. Sqdn marched such to ANTOING where off Trps.	

Army Form C. 2118.

WAR DIARY
or
INTELLIGENCE SUMMARY
(Erase heading not required.)

Instructions regarding War Diaries and Intelligence Summaries are contained in F.S. Regs., Part II. and the Staff Manual respectively. Title pages will be prepared in manuscript. Ref 1/100,000 Sheets 11.12.5.6.

Sheet III

November 1918

Place	Date	Hour	Summary of Events and Information	Remarks and references to Appendices
	11th		Troops rejoined HQrs & Section for R&R returned in R&R areas. Many road mines were removed during the day from roads in line of march.	C/C
	12th		Sqdn marched to VERON (Sheet 5) Div Conference at 14.00 hrs at [illeg] relating to "2LH" & "Polish" were received - in addition to particulars in Div files forward to frontier. Sqdn employed in removing mines in Div area.	
	13th		B Ech rejoined	
	16th		2nd Troop joined 4th Bde	
	17th		1st Troop joined 6th Bde	
	18th		Sqdn HQrs & troops marched to HELLE BECQ (Sheet 5) Cav. Corps Bdge Section left to rejoin its Unit.	
	19th		Sqdn moved to PETIT-ENGHIEN. The Division have continued movement - mines and a great deal of work was done in removing same. In addition the Railways radiating from ENGHIEN in all directions were mined with charge whilst using 35' of the railway was released. In one instance with R.E. of 2nd & 4th Div, for several miles. The road bridge in and around ENGHIEN was examined and reported safe. 10 Heavy shells were removed from Road Bridge on railway at 13/4 km W of ATH-ENGHIEN road. (Sheet 6)	
	19th		At SAINTES (6th R&R Sheet) mines were removed from railway bridge S.W. of FRANCOIS (Sheet 6) Sqdn was also employed in removal of mines in & around PETIT ENGHIEN (Sheet 6) River at TUBIZE had been dammed with logs - presumably with intention of inundating surrounding country. This dam was removed with explosives and water reduced by H. Fuzy (Sheet 6)	
	20th		Mines removed from railway line from [illeg] west of MUSSAIN station (Sheet 6)	

Army Form C. 2118.

Sheet IV

FIELD SQUADRON R.E.
November 1918

WAR DIARY
INTELLIGENCE SUMMARY
(Erase heading not required.)

Ref 1/100,000 Sheets 11.12. 5.6.

Place	Date	Hour	Summary of Events and Information	Remarks and references to Appendices
	20th		Over 100 shells were removed. Bdy over canal 1 Km S.E of TUBIZE Station were the shanged - large quantities of H.E. had been placed in retaliation to the 16 heavy shells.	
	21st		Sqdn moved to WATERLOO	
	22nd		Sqdn moved to PERWEZ	
	25th		Mines were removed from railway station just E of NAMUR by 1st Troop attached to 6th Cav Bde.	

OFFICERS. Transfers, etc.

Capt. J. S. Kidders, R.A.M.C. rejoined unit from Cav. Corps Equitation School. 5-11-18
2/Lt. R. R. Young, R.E. Joined unit from R.E. Base Depot 14.11.18
2/Lt. R. R. Young. R.E. admitted to hospital 24.11.18.

Major, R.E.

3rd Cav Fd Sqn

War Diary for Dec.
herewith

H.S. Macnachin
Lt RE
for
O.C. 3rd Field Sq R.E.

WAR DIARY 3rd (Fd) Squadron R.E.
INTELLIGENCE SUMMARY

Army Form C. 2118.

December - 1918

Place	Date	Hour	Summary of Events and Information	Remarks and references to Appendices
	Dec 1918 1		Squadron moved to TOURINNES - ST-LAMBERT remained up to 15th - all extra time given over to sports & recreation	
	15		Squadron moved to AINEFFE	
	16		" " to OUGREE - nothing able to get in at TILF	
	17		" " to SCLESSIN. Remained to end of month. Army strength sickness & demobilisation squadron reduced to 3 horses throughout to 1 man. 146 A.T. Coy & 221 A.T. Coy allotted to 3rd W. Car. Divn for work in Dinan Area arrived at SERAIN on 17th. 146 A.T. Coy employed on Workshop and work North East end of area. 221 A.T. Coy to be moved to West end of area.	

Officers, fears, casualties, etc.
2/Lt. Young R.R. admitted to hospital 24.11.18.
2/Lt. Young R.R. returned from hospital 2.12.18
Lt. Macomochie D. leave to U.K extended from 15½ to 6½ Auth W.O.575.

C Rawson
Cmdg 3 W Fd Sqn RE

3rd FIELD SQUADRON R.E.
Army Form C. 2118.

Jan'y 1919

WAR DIARY
or
INTELLIGENCE SUMMARY.
(Erase heading not required.)

Vol 49

Place	Date	Hour	Summary of Events and Information	Remarks and references to Appendices
SCLESSIN BELGIUM	January 1919		Work in Div. Area:- (i) Fitting out Corps Concentration Camp at SERAING and fitting out P & R T School RAMET (ii) Making field latrines incinerators and other camp appliances and erecting same in Div Area (iii) Lorry loading ramp constructed at ENGIS (iv) Animal Collecting Station at ENGIS - work on this was carried out by 146 A.T Coy R.E (attd 3rd Cav. Div) (v) 221 A T Coy left about 3 P.M. for NAMUR to work with 9th Army as there was not enough work in the 3rd Cav. Div area to retain two W.T. Coys. (vi) Recruiting. Officer Casualties I Lt Bagsley R.F.A R.E School 29-1-19 E 2nd Lt RicHardson R.E demobilized ″ ‶ III 2nd Lt Young R.E ″ ″ ″ R. J. Macauley Capt. R.E. O.C 3rd Field Sqdn R.E 17-2-19	

3rd Field Sqdr. R.E.

FIELD SQUADRON R.E.
Army Form C. 2118.

Vol 50

WAR DIARY
or
INTELLIGENCE SUMMARY.

February 1919

(Erase heading not required.)

Instructions regarding War Diaries and Intelligence Summaries are contained in F.S. Regs., Part II. and the Staff Manual respectively. Title pages will be prepared in manuscript.

Place	Date	Hour	Summary of Events and Information	Remarks and references to Appendices
ÉCLESSIN BELGIUM	1st to 15th		Work Parties employed in construction of Water-troughs etc at Z Horse Depot SERAING, general carpenters work at COCKERILLS Works, snow-ploughs and other general carpenters work at P.O.W. Camp. — This 10 N.C.O's & men sent to ENGIS for work and work were employed in field erection of huts and hut work involved. The work for standing horses at ENGIS was taken over & reconstructed. Work was commenced on Delousing chamber at CONCENTRATION CAMP-SERAING	
	19th		Work was commenced on Delousing chamber at CONCENTRATION CAMP-SERAING. Instructed to the instructions of D.A.R.M. 2nd Corps Div. Sign-boards were made and painted &c. for on hand for P.O.W.	
	20th		Ablution-Benches-latrines-Cupboards etc. for on hand for P.O.W. Camp at JEMEPPE.	
	21st		Work on P.O.W Camp ENGIS was finished.	
	24th		Work in hand :- Alterations to P.O.W. Camp at JEMEPPE. Construction of Latrines. Incinerators. Ablution Benches- Cupboards for P.O.W. Camp JEMEPPE	
	28th		During the month demobilisation of men and horses proceeded many of the Asst Remainder were kept in readiness awaiting orders- Checking equipment etc and general routine of the month. The following casualties not to be reported during the month :-	

I Demobilisation : { 2/27 Richardson, F. to CONCENT 1/2/19
{ 2/27 Young, R.R. to do 15/2/19
II Transfers : - 1/27 CRAWHALL T.C joined from 1st Field Sqdr. 15/2/19
O.R. to CONCENT during month 31.

W.J.M Warmoth Capt. R.E
O.C 3rd Field Sqdr. R.E

3 Cdn

Army Form C. 2118.

3rd Field Squadron R.E.

WAR DIARY for MARCH 1919

or

INTELLIGENCE SUMMARY.

(Erase heading not required.)

Instructions regarding War Diaries and Intelligence Summaries are contained in F.S. Regs., Part II. and the Staff Manual respectively. Title pages will be prepared in manuscript.

Place	Date	Hour	Summary of Events and Information	Remarks and references to Appendices
SCLESSIN LIEGE	1st		Work — P.O.W. Camp JEMEPPE	
	7th		Orders received that Squadron mounted from host of Cavalry Division of occupation.	
	10th		Warned to collect to Cadre B for ENGLAND. Released orders to reduce to Cadre A.	
	13th		Month was spent in chiefly stores by Held Store Liege. Repairing and overhauling wagons and equipment.	
			General Routine.	
			Casualties	
			Lt. Othermedu rejoined from France leave. Major C.F. Cansh rejoined Ghent from leave in UK. Major C.F. Cansh left Units to transit to England for leave. Lt. B.O.R. and Lt. Amero rest of 14th Sqdn in route for Eng. At Cadre of Evacuation (Special leave to U.K. (5 again 15th at Maubeuge Repatriated to B.E.F.) (on 16.3.19) Field Squadron return to B.E.F. (on 24.19)	
			DEMOBILIZATION during month: 33 O.R. 9 CONCENTRATION CAMP	

Army Form C. 2118.

332 Field Squadron RE   April 1919

WAR DIARY
or
INTELLIGENCE SUMMARY.
(Erase heading not required.)

Instructions regarding War Diaries and Intelligence Summaries are contained in F. S. Regs., Part II. and the Staff Manual respectively. Title pages will be prepared in manuscript.

Place	Date	Hour	Summary of Events and Information	Remarks and references to Appendices
Schoven	14.19		Orders for the probable entrainment of cadres for part of squadron between the 5th and 7th were received on 28.3.19. Embarkation roll giving further instructions for despatch of our cadres confirmed. Pending further instructions for despatch of U.K. wagons were separated and equipment overhauled and repacked.	
			Demobilization 1 Other rank was demobilized during month.	
	30.4.19		**Transfers** Major R.J. Alexander R.E. departed to HQ.IV on 28.4.19 to take up duties of CRE Siege Sch. Area. Lieut. H.D. Macorochie R.E. left unit for 332. Field Company on 29.4.19.	
			A/C On departure of Major Alexander, 2/Lieut. T.C. Santallier took over duties of A/OC 332 Fld. Sq. R.E.	

L. Marshall
2/Lieut. RE
A/OC 332 Field Squadron RE
8.5.19

CENTRAL REGISTRY
HEADQUARTERS
WIMEREUX.
10 JUN 1919

3rd
FIELD SQUADRON
R.E.
8-6-19

G.O.C. British Tps in France & Flanders

Herewith War Diary for Month
of May 1919.

O.C. 3rd Field Squadron R.E.

3rd FIELD SQUADRON R.E.
Army Form C. 2118.

G.O.C.
B.T. in F & F

WAR DIARY
INTELLIGENCE SUMMARY
for Month of May 1919.

Vol 53

(Erase heading not required.)

Place	Date	Hour	Summary of Events and Information	Remarks and references to Appendices
Solesmes	1st		Routine work	
"	20th		2/Lt Cantrell to Hospital	
"	20th		Lt Parish joined for duty	
	22nd		Squadron moved to Huy	
Huy			24 O.R. were demobilised during the month	

R Parish Lt R.E.
O.C. 3rd Field Squadron R.E.

www.ingramcontent.com/pod-product-compliance
Lightning Source LLC
Chambersburg PA
CBHW081537160426
43191CB00011B/1777